# IGNORE YOUR CUSTOMERS

## (AND THEY'LL GO AWAY)

# IGNORE YOUR CUSTOMERS

AND THEY'LL

GO AWAY

**THE SIMPLE PLAYBOOK
FOR DELIVERING THE
ULTIMATE CUSTOMER
SERVICE EXPERIENCE**

# MICAH SOLOMON

HARPERCOLLINS
LEADERSHIP

AN IMPRINT OF HARPERCOLLINS

*For everyone who works to delight customers every day.*

# CONTENTS

# FOREWORD

*Ignore Your Customers (And They'll Go Away)* is a superbly enjoyable read: clever, witty, and oftentimes laugh-out-loud funny (which is not what you'd expect from your run-of-the-mill business book). But don't let the light tone mislead you. What the engaging author—renowned customer service consultant and speaker Micah Solomon—is talking about here is heart-attack serious. *It can make all the difference to your bottom line.*

It's been our experience at Safelite AutoGlass, year after year, that following the game plan Micah lays out in these pages—particularly around the three key themes of improving customer service, fine-tuning the customer experience, and improving the employee experience—can lead to doubling, even tripling, of our financial success metrics, and that this can be accomplished even in the face of challenging economic times and factors.

You should be sure to take to heart the author's other pointers as well: avoiding the "cliff of dissatisfaction" (this is when you're not up to the speed demanded by customers, and they lose faith in you as a result), learning to serve the important and challenging millennial generation, building the systems and standards essential to reliably and repeatably serve your customers, and building a true customer service culture.

(About this last subject, culture: there's nothing that's more important than the issue of company culture, and there's no guide better able to lead you to success here than Micah.)

At Safelite, Micah's plan is in our DNA, and we define it as being people powered and customer driven. This is encompassed in the three characteristics of what we call our Safelite Spirit: a service mindset, can-do attitude, and caring heart. When you put people first, everything else falls into place—and you achieve extraordinary results.

Turn the page. It's time to start this wonderful journey with Micah.

—Tom Feeney, President and CEO,
Safelite AutoGlass

# PREFACE

A t JetBlue, we often refer to ourselves as a *customer service company that just happens to fly airplanes.*

In the spring of 1999, before we named the airline or even knew which planes we would purchase, we knew we wanted to offer a better experience than customers were receiving across the industry. It didn't take us long to create our mission—To Bring Humanity Back to Air Travel, and, since our first flight in February 2000, we've been striving to inspire humanity one customer at a time via what we call the "JetBlue Experience," an experience that is upheld and supported by multiple pillars that we must continually focus on day in and day out.

*The first pillar of the JetBlue Experience is crewmember (employee) recruitment:* hiring the right crewmembers who possess a strong desire to serve others and to create personalized and meaningful interactions. This is essential for two reasons: First because their unique, individual, and caring approach to hospitality truly powers the experience, and second because they inspire each other and future crewmembers as well.

*The second pillar is mindset—or as Micah calls it in chapter 2, culture.* Mindset and culture, of course, come from both the bottom and the top. Proper crewmember selection is essential here, but so is complete buy-in, all the way up to the CEO. Every company *has* a culture; the question is: Are you fostering the *right* culture, the culture you desire? What is the mindset across all levels within your organization?

*The third pillar is a technology-driven, innovative approach.* JetBlue was the first in our industry to have a contact center that was 100 percent home-based, giving our customer support crewmembers the flexibility to work from home, because we believe happier crewmembers translate into happier and more loyal customers. We were also one of the first airlines to use social platforms to engage with our customers. Regardless of the channel where we engage with customers, we do so via the most appropriate technology possible, notably a conversational platform provided by Gladly that we first launched in 2017, that keeps all of our customer conversations housed in a single view regardless of the communication channel, oftentimes eliminating the need for customers to repeat themselves. Overall, this helps us create meaningful relationships rather than treating our customers like a ticket number.

*And the fourth pillar, just as essential as the other three, is training and lifelong learning.* And here is where Micah Solomon's long customer service consulting career, and the unique book you're holding, come in. *Ignore Your Customers (And They'll Go Away)* introduces, stresses, and amplifies the essentials of the JetBlue Experience through the lens of some of the greatest companies of our time, as well as via Micah's truly unique perspective and tenured experience.

I hope that as you read *Ignore Your Customers (And They'll Go Away)*, you'll think of it from the perspective of companies like JetBlue, where we strive to be *humane* the way Micah counsels; *efficient*—so customers never fall off what Micah memorably calls "the cliff of dissatisfaction"; and, wherever possible, to *pursue anticipatory customer service*, which he speaks so eloquently about in these pages. Please, also, be careful not to skim through the pages and paragraphs that discuss *diversity and inclusion*. These are essential, central principles at JetBlue and I hope they are—or soon will be—at your organization as well.

And do consider us for your next flight; we'll be pleased to hear how we at JetBlue hold up to Micah's principles. Don't hesitate to share your experience with us, and be candid, because we're always striving to learn and improve.

—Frankie Littleford, Vice President, Customer Support,
Experience, Operations, and Recovery, JetBlue

# AUTHOR'S NOTE:
# THE BEST JOB IN THE WORLD (MINE!)

B eing a mystery shopper is harder than it looks. (*"Sure, Micah, sure it is."*)

Bear with me and I'll explain.

When, say, a luxury hotel hires me to revamp their customer service, I often start by going undercover.

It's loads of fun, of course. But the challenges are unique.

For example: When I'm at the hotel's boutique spa getting a facial (for research, of course!) and have both eyes covered by cucumber slices, it's a real magic trick finding a discreet time to peek out and observe the customer service interactions that are going on around me. And it's just as difficult to take notes on the sly while submitting to a massage or a mani or a pedi.

(I do draw the line at getting waxed, even for professional reasons.)

Not all of my workdays are equally glamorous, as a customer service consultant/mystery shopper/customer service keynote speaker/customer experience designer/customer service trainer (there are a lot of slashes in my job title). It's just as likely that you'll find me onsite at a law office, retail store, financial services firm, insurance agency, plumbing supply company, or—no kidding—a mortuary. Regardless of the setting, though, I'm doing essentially the same work: evaluating the customer experience and polishing the customer service until it shines. And even though I sometimes like to complain (I am a professional fault-finder, after all), I know that I *do* have the greatest job, the greatest work life, that I could imagine.

This isn't just business to me. *I love this stuff.* I love helping businesses rethink their relationships with customers, I love contributing to their prospects for sustained success, and I love seeing the ultimate results.

I intend to be a good companion and guide to you throughout these pages, and I appreciate that you've chosen to join me here. If you'd like to reach me for more direct assistance, I invite you to do that as well. Please email me at micah@micahsolomon.com or text or call me on my phone, (484) 343-5881, if you're struggling with a particularly thorny customer service problem or customer experience conundrum that could benefit from my involvement. (You can also use the live chat feature that you can find front and center on my website, micahsolomon.com, which will connect you with me directly—and it's me who does the chatting, not a robotic, simulated Micah.)

# SHOOT FOR THE MOON: WHY THE HIGHEST LEVEL OF CUSTOMER SERVICE IS THE ONLY ONE WORTH AIMING FOR

When the Guruphone rings (it's like the Batphone, but for consultants) and I slide down my firepole to assist, the call is often from a business that was once thriving but has since lost its way with customers and needs help turning the relationship around. The first thing I do after arriving onsite is to pore through whatever records and relics I can find from those earlier, happier days, looking for hints as to what might have changed. What I'll find, nearly invariably, are clues suggesting that the care taken with customers in those early, golden days was superior to what's going on now in a variety of predictable ways: the level of personalization in each customer interaction, the number of customer follow-ups and the care invested in each one, the thought that went into hiring, and other similar key markers.

Unfortunately, the focus and attentiveness that are common when a business has only a few customers tend to slide when the customer roster begins to balloon. Employees stop signing their thank-you notes by hand. Managers busy themselves with paperwork in their office hideaways rather than coming out into the open to greet even longtime or VIP customers—and they're certainly nowhere to be found if a customer conflict ever erupts and needs smoothing over.

Jackie and Joanne, the quirky, charismatic telephone operators who knew the name and backstory of every customer who called in, are edged into retirement and replaced (although, in reality, they're irreplaceable) with low-paid rookies or a voice jail system.

Is such lowering of standards inevitable? Decidedly not—if you stubbornly stick to your guns. The mantra that's needed is this: *If you would've done something for your first customer, you'll find a way to keep doing it for your ten thousandth,* without rushing, without cutting corners, and without doing anything that would make a customer feel less than fully valued by your business.

The secret, in other words, is to *never stop believing in the importance of the individual customer* and the importance of every individual interaction, no matter how many customers your organization has grown to serve. Don't fall into the trap of thinking there's an infinite supply of new customers out there for the taking if only your marketing and sales departments would do their jobs, seeking out and converting more leads. Tell yourself instead that not only are customers a limited commodity, there's *no such thing as "customers" in the plural.* Rather, there's just one customer: the one who's being served right now.

Advocating and sustaining this attitude of treating each customer like the only one in the world is one of the most important leadership responsibilities in any organization, and it's one of the key weapons in the battle to avoid losing customers through perceived (and, perhaps, actual) indifference.

If you *do* neglect your customers, it's probably going to hurt *you* more than it hurts them. In most every industry today, there are scores of businesses eager and able to accommodate any customer of yours whom you inadvertently send their way through your neglect.

But enough with the negatives. I'm too much of a natural optimist to stay in this fearmonger role for long. And the ultimate reason I want you to develop or renew your customer focus is much more positive. It's that customer-by-customer excellence is the best way to build a business, sustain a business, and reach for the stars.

It's also the most **cost-effective** way to grow your business. For comparison: *How much did you spend on marketing last year? Advertising? Sales?* Developing a true customer focus is far and away the most effective, affordable way to keep the revenue flowing. And the secrets of doing just that? You now hold them here in your hands.

## WHY I USE "THEY" IN THIS BOOK, RATHER THAN "HE OR SHE"

In this book, you'll find I use "they" instead of he/she as the gender in hypothetical sentences. This is in keeping with the latest AP style guidelines. I also intend it as an acknowledgment of the people who prefer "they" as their pronoun.

## Chapter by Chapter: What You'll Learn in This Book

Throughout this book, I'll be both your instructor and your cheerleader, helping you avoid the missteps that lead to alienated customers and showing you the positive steps that will put you on track to surpass your competition. Here's a glimpse of what I'll be covering in the pages to come.

In **chapter 1**, I'll push you (maybe a bit maniacally) to create an ideal state at your company that I call "**automatic positivity**," where the answer to any customer question is *expected* to be yes. As a bonus, we'll spend time in this chapter with Tony Hsieh, the innovative CEO of Zappos, to see how this default of positivity plays out in the Zappos world.

In **chapter 2**, I'll start by defining "**customer service culture**," and then we'll get to work building a superior one for your own organization. This is fundamental, essential work.

In **chapter 3**, I'll dig into the all-important subject of **talent management**: the selection, care, and nurturing of employees. We'll look at the mindset and methodologies that will equip you to successfully recruit, select, and get the most out of the employees who power your company and its relationship with customers.

In **chapter 4**, we'll focus on creating **"wow" customer experiences**, looking at how these moments of wow come about and where they can lead a company, its customers, and its employees. This chapter isn't all platitudes and happy talk; we'll look at the serious work and hard-to-achieve corporate mindset required to make these magical moments happen (and even delineate the occasions—there are some—where trying to wow a customer might be the wrong strategy).

In **chapter 5**, we'll look at **the *experience* part of the customer experience**, taking a visit to Drybar, the coast-to-coast "blowout bar" salon phenomenon that has grown from just one to 125 locations over the course of a very few years, and look at how Drybar manages to impart emotional resonance to the most mundane of acts: blow-drying a client's hair. We'll also look briefly at one of the world's legendary healthcare institutions, the Mayo Clinic, which has done great work on improving the customer (patient) experience in this most serious of settings.

In **chapter 6**, I'll show you **how to *consistently* deliver great customer service by creating essential standards and systems**. Although the subject may sound unsexy, this chapter contains some of the most important lessons in this book.

We'll kick off **chapter 7** by visiting with Sir Richard Branson, who will help us dig into the dangers of "**Stepford Customer Service**." This feeds into the chapter's theme: how to shake the cobwebs and artifice from your customer service approach and create **an authentic style of service**: one that avoids repelling customers through excessive formality and other cues that convey insincerity.

Customers are a moving target, and the customer landscape has been changing rapidly, particularly since the advent of the digital communications revolution. While this is an undercurrent that runs through much of this book, it's the particular focus of **chapter 8**. Here we'll look at **how digital communications and the accelerating pace of consumer life have changed the expectations of your customers**, and I'll provide pointers on how to successfully align the customer experience with these new realities.

Every hour that they're awake, customers and prospects are busy sharing their opinions and impressions of your business. **Chapter 9** takes a look at how the hypersocial inclinations of today's customers are affecting your business and **how to make the most of these social connections** to influence purchasing decisions and overall customer happiness.

Moving on to **chapter 10**, I explain how to avoid the hazards of the deadly **cliff of dissatisfaction**: the point at which customers lose patience with your company's speed of service. If you fail to keep customers away from this death-dealing cliff, there's no amount of warmth and empathy and no number of heartfelt apologies that can ever entirely compensate.

This brings us to the **ominously numbered chapter 11**,\* where I briefly wrap things up.

## Getting the Most from This Book

If you want to absorb and retain as much as possible of what you're about to read, here's my suggested approach.

1. **Read it with your team at work.** The best way to get the full benefit is to read *Ignore Your Customers (And They'll Go Away)* as part of a group. Get your colleagues and direct reports and, yes, your bosses, to read it together with you. A book is a super-affordable way to get five

---

\* Poor old Chapter 7 has a similar problem.

or fifty or five thousand people on the same page; it's what the term "on the same page" is all about. As legendary business thinker Seth Godin puts it, "Books are vessels for ideas, but the ideas in them are most likely to change people and organizations when they're spoken out loud and when promises and commitments are made."

2. **Make use of the "Get to the Point, Micah!"** *Cliffs-Notes*-**style cheatsheets that you'll find at the end of each chapter to help you review what's been covered.** Make notes and highlights here as well as you see fit.

3. **Ask your team at work the questions in the Reading Group Guide that's included at the end of each chapter.** Answer out loud and have someone take notes. (If, on the other hand, you're reading by yourself in a shared space, proceed with caution on the "answer out loud" part.)

4. **Pay attention to the "Diversity and Inclusion Notes."** They are at the ends of chapter 3 (provided by diversity guru Michael Hyter, Managing Partner at Korn Ferry and author of *The Power of Inclusion*) and chapter 5 (provided by Jan Jones Blackhurst, Caesars International Board of Directors, former Caesars Vice President for Public Policy and Corporate Responsibility and the first female mayor of Las Vegas).

5. **Mark it up!—unless it's a copy from the library.** I'll be flattered rather than offended if you mark up this book, unless your comments are catty and I discover your copy for sale later on eBay. If you're reading an e-book, you can do something similar to marking up a physical book by making use of the highlighting/ notes function and then digitally filing, or printing out, your highlights and notes when you're done.

6. **When you've reached the end of the book, review your notes and your highlighted passages and scan the chapter cheatsheets one final time.** Then file your takeaways somewhere that you're sure to see them again. (My personal approach to doing this is inelegant but effective: I paste the most valuable nuggets from the books I've read on every available surface of my office. It's a ludicrously messy way of working, but I always know where to find the stuff that matters to me.)

## A Glimpse of the Payoff

What I'm going to challenge you to do in this book isn't easy: to build an organization that is centered on your customers in fundamental yet sophisticated ways. But it will be an incredibly fruitful venture, resulting in a multipart payoff:

- You'll retain a higher proportion of your existing customers . . .
- You'll increase per-customer spending . . .
- You'll attract new customers . . .

. . . and you'll do it all in a way that is *almost entirely immune to being knocked off by competitors.*

If this last claim, "immune to knockoff," sounds farfetched, let me explain and defend my reasoning. I'm making this claim because I have a strong hunch that if you do the work suggested in this book, you can sleep easy knowing that it's unlikely that your competition will buckle down and do the same. Although your competition may copy your pricing, ape your innovations, duplicate the look and feel of your website, and so forth, they're unlikely to muster the vision, energy, and follow-through required to replicate the customer-centered organization that I'm here to help you build.

I'm not going to pretend that the fruits of your labor will fall off the vine and into your hands overnight. As a businessperson myself, I know all about the challenges of getting through the grind of making payroll week by week while striving to move forward strategically. But I know it can be done, and I've done it time and again for the companies I work with. The serious stakes I play for are the growth, improved profitability, and ultimate survival of the companies and business leaders for whom I consult, train, and speak.

Which now, through the magic of the printed word, include you. Let's get to work.

# IGNORE YOUR CUSTOMERS

## (AND THEY'LL GO AWAY)

# AUTOMATIC POSITIVITY

*Stop me if you've heard this one already.* An agent in the Zappos call center once spent a staggering amount of time (ten hours and twenty-nine minutes) on the telephone with a customer who'd called in for help deciding on the perfect pair of Uggs. This topped even the previous record at Zappos, a similarly jaw-dropping eight hours and forty-seven minutes.

The ten-plus hour Zappos phone call quickly became legendary. Late-night host Jimmy Fallon even covered it in a human-interest segment where he brought in an actor to play the Zappos employee, whom he then united on air with the Uggs-seeking customer.

When I first heard about the marathon Zappos phone call, there was one detail missing that I felt compelled to track down, so I put the question to Zappos CEO Tony Hsieh the first chance I got.

*Did the employee get a bathroom break? For that matter, did the customer?*

I wish I'd used my wristwatch to time the silence that followed, but eventually Tony (who had clearly expected a different line of questioning) responded.

"I'm not actually sure," he told me, peering back from beneath his new Mohawk hairdo—the first Mohawk I'd seen on a gainfully employed master of the universe. Eventually, Jamie Naughton, the Zappos chief of staff, rescued the conversation by confirming that both the Zappos employee and the customer on the other end of the line did, in fact, take breaks in the course of the phone call to use the bathroom.

"Well, that's good news—but, even with empty bladders," I persisted, "what did they talk about for ten hours? Was it really Uggs for all that time?"

Tony looked at me with growing exasperation. "They talked about whatever friends would talk about."

Point taken.

And even more to the point: Although talking with a customer for ten straight hours is indefensible by traditional call center logic (where a call is supposed to only take five to eight minutes) it makes business sense if you think of the ten-hour phone call as a flag that Zappos has hoisted high in the air to illustrate to its employees just how far they should be ready to go to make an emotional connection with a customer.

The marathon call is now an important part of Zappos company lore, akin to the tire-refund legend at Nordstrom: an illustration that no matter what a customer wants from an agent at Zappos, it's the agent's job to make sure that the customer gets it, even if it takes ten hours.

And twenty-nine minutes.

## Automatic Positivity

Don't worry; the way that I myself go about building great, customer-oriented companies does *not* require indulging in ten-hour phone calls à la Zappos, but it does require that you apply focus, passion, and even theatricality (a Zappos specialty) to create what I call "automatic positivity." This is where an organization's go-to position is to say yes to customer requests, rather than defaulting to an easy "no" or one of the many synonyms for no.

In other words, here's the sentiment that should be on the tip of every employee tongue, straining to come out:

*The answer is yes! Now what was your question?*

That you should strive to tell your customers "yes" might seem self-evident. Yet a single misguided employee can easily find a dozen opportunities, every single shift, to say no to your customers. That is why it's essential that employees get the message from their leaders, loud and clear, that the goal is to try to find a way to accommodate their customers, whether or not a manager is around to approve it.

## When Your Attempts to Say Yes Slam into Reality

But what happens when an attempt to say yes slams into the obstacles that inevitably come up in the rough-and-tumble world of serving customers, the scenarios where the answer must in fact be no? When this is the case, there's almost always a way to soften the blow.

The solution, generally, is to restrain yourself from delivering this final no without having a yes to offer in the same breath. Offer an alternative solution and an apology that is likely to make your "no" easier to accept: "I'm sorry, Mr. Henderson. Although we are unable to ship all eight pieces of luggage you ordered on our website to Madagascar without charge, would it help if we shipped the suitcase you plan on giving to your wife overnight at our expense?"

Look at the lengths that Joanne Hassis, a salesperson *par excellence* at Nordstrom, will go to avoid disappointing a customer (i.e., me) with a "no." Not long ago, my favorite short-sleeve shirts, which I had been buying from Nordstrom for years, were discontinued by Nordstrom's supplier, and, as a result, Joanne was no longer able to sell them to me. Rather than just saying, "Sorry, Micah—that'll be a no," she found a solution, even though it came from a competing site with private label shirts that Joanne felt would work as a substitute. While this didn't make any money directly for Joanne or Nordstrom, you can bet that I'm now more faithful than ever about buying the rest of my wardrobe from Joanne—and about recommending her services to others as well. (As, in fact, I've done here.)

## HEALTH, SAFETY, AND SECURITY EXCEPTIONS TO "YES"

There is a set of scenarios where you shouldn't even be trying to get to yes. This is when the request has risky safety, health, or security implications.

So, please don't misapply this chapter's advice in any of the following ways:

- "Sure, I'll bypass our passcode verification procedures and get you into your account, since you've forgotten your password."
- "Feel free to keep drinking at our bar far beyond the point of sobriety."
- "Yeah, that's fine if you prop open our swimming pool safety gate to make load-in and load-out easier for your kid's birthday party."
- "We don't mind if you move your chair in front of that marked emergency exit."
- "I'll be happy to drive you to the airport even though I've had a few after-work drinks."

. . . and so forth.

Though providing alternatives if you have to say no is important in every industry, in the hospitality industry it's *officially required behavior* at any hotel that is striving to achieve a rating of five stars from *Forbes*. At Ocean House, a double five-star (Forbes-rated), double five-diamond (AAA rated) resort in Rhode Island, situations where they aren't able to deliver a yes to a guest are rare indeed, but here's a hypothetical one: a guest wanting to have breakfast in their restaurant when the hour is pushing noon. I asked Daniel Hostettler, the president of Ocean House, how he would handle this situation: "First off, we wouldn't tell them the dining area is closed unless absolutely necessary. And if that *is* necessary, we would offer to serve them by the fireplace in the living room area, or on the outdoor verandah, if the weather is suitable."

Even when the "no" is due to external circumstances rather than the limitations of their property, Hostettler's team tries to create "alternative yeses" to accommodate their guests.

Not long ago, the Ocean House staff learned that a couple was headed their way who had planned to honeymoon in the Caribbean until their intended destination was all but destroyed in a hurricane. As a consolation, the couple was redirecting their travel plans to the Rhode Island coast for a non tropical, but just as beachy, honeymoon trip. Hostettler and staff anticipated the couple's arrival by gathering sand and seashells from the hotel's own beach (a chilly task—it was November in New England), digging two margaritas into the sand and placing the resulting tableau on the nightstand with a note that read, "We're bringing the Caribbean to you," further setting the scene with calypso music on the guestroom sound system, intended to put the couple in a tropical mood when they walked in.

## HOW ONE TECH COMPANY MODELS AUTOMATIC POSITIVITY BY SAYING YES EVEN TO *NON*-CUSTOMERS

Tomas Gorny, cofounder and CEO of Nextiva, one of the fastest-growing business communications companies in the US, tells me that in order to make sure his employees are delivering Amazing Service (a concept so central to the company that they've actually trademarked the term; I've looked it up: it's US Trademark # 4574257), Gorny encourages his team to provide amazing service even to people who aren't, realistically speaking, prospects, people with no current ability to use Nextiva's services.

Here's how far Nextiva will go to provide support even to those who aren't yet customers: When a tweet appeared in Nextiva's twitter feed asking about a service Nextiva didn't even offer (VoIP service in a particular country overseas), within minutes a response appeared back from Nextiva—and it wasn't simply a reply tweet, like, "Thanks for asking. But no!"

Rather, an employee took it upon himself to fire up a video camera and send, as his response, an engaging, brief video explaining why the company doesn't offer this at present in their service area and thanking them for their inquiry. Needless to say, the original tweeter was floored, as, I expect, was every Twitter user who noticed the exchange.

## How to Build Automatic Positivity

If you want to work toward a default position of yes in your company or department, start by supporting "yes behavior" in the following ways.

- **Model "yes behavior" yourself.** If you aren't willing to make yes *your* default, why should anyone else? Be aware of what comes out of your own mouth when employees are listening, and of how you behave when they are watching. If you hear yourself frequently telling customers some version of, "I'm afraid we cannot accommodate that request," your employees will follow suit and find opportunities to likewise refuse to accommodate customers.

- **Spell out your commitment to yes.** Write the default of yes (including the nuances of what to do when you *can't* say yes) into your company standards—and *publicize* those standards throughout the company.

- **Preach the gospel of defaulting to yes, starting in the very first minutes of employment.** Make it clear, from the first days of an employee's tenure, that the way things are done around here is with customer-focused flexibility; that working here involves an ongoing attempt to maintain, in almost all situations, a default of yes. Then, continue to remind employees about the importance of "yes" in your daily Customer Service Minute (see chapter 2) and via any other creative means you can think of.
- **Support your employees in getting to yes.** From their first fledgling, awkward attempts to find a yes for customers to their later, more-refined performances, employee efforts at yes deserve encouragement and applause.

## THE DANGER OF SITUATIONAL TYRANTS: THE "NO MONSTERS" WHO CAN SABOTAGE A COMPANY'S BEST EFFORTS

While most anti-yes behavior is served up by well-intentioned, if misguided, employees, there is a more unsavory scenario to watch out for. Any organization or department can become a breeding ground for what I call *situational tyrants*—employees who have the power to say no within their tiny fiefdoms, and who exercise that power every chance they get. When a customer is looking for even a tiny bit of flexibility, a situational tyrant will slam the rulebook down with sadistic glee.

Here are four ways to avoid breeding and empowering situational tyrants.

1. **Hire appropriately.** Strive to select applicants for customer-facing positions who have the requisite personality traits for superior customer service. (More on this in chapter 3.)
2. **Don't misunderstand, and don't let your employees misunderstand, empowerment.** The kind of empowerment that great

companies embrace (see chapter 4) shouldn't be misinterpreted as a license to kiss off a challenging or "noncompliant" (as they say in healthcare) customer. On the contrary, the kind of empowerment you should be encouraging employees to exercise should almost always be *in favor of* a customer. Going *against* the customer, if it's necessary, should require deliberation and team or management involvement. Consider adopting Commerce Bank's approach: "It takes one employee to say yes, two to say no."

3. **Trust but verify.** The way that a situational tyrant behaves in the presence of a person in power, such as a company leader, may be far different from how they act when they're out of earshot of the boss, especially if the tyrant's alone with a customer whom they believe to be powerless. So, it's important for leaders to have an ear to the ground, listening to what other employees may be saying, since a leader may have trouble witnessing and uncovering situational tyranny themselves. And once you *do* witness the tyrannical behavior, it's essential to act quickly, as your other employees will be watching for your response.

4. **Counsel (very directly, if necessary).** Some tyrannical employees will never recognize the need to change until you're extraordinarily direct with them. I wouldn't rush to assume that any employee is permanently set in their tyrannical ways until you lay things out for them in black and white. And this way, if they do fail to improve after the situation is made clear to them, at least you'll know you gave them every opportunity.

One final note: it's outside the scope of this chapter, but *situational tyranny in the treatment of employees by a supervisor* is a similar, and similarly serious, problem in many organizations.

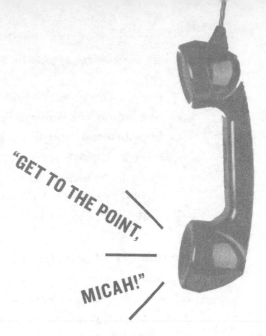

**"GET TO THE POINT, MICAH!"**

# READER'S CHEATSHEET FOR CHAPTER 1

The default employee attitude in a customer-focused organization should be, **"The answer is yes! Now what was your question?"** rather than defaulting to no and its variants.

**When you can't say yes:** In scenarios where the answer must in fact be no, there's almost always a way to soften the "no blow." Try not to say no without having a reasonable alternative to offer.

*IMPORTANT NOTE: There is a category of scenarios where you shouldn't even be trying to get to yes.* ***This is when saying yes to a request has potential safety, health, or security implications.***

**How to build automatic positivity:** Here are ways to build support for a default of yes:

- **Spell it out.** Write the default of yes into your company standards and publicize it throughout your organization.

- **Preach the gospel of defaulting to yes, starting with new-employee onboarding.**
- **Support your employees in getting there.** Employee efforts at yes deserve applause—and require it, if the yeses aren't going to fade out as quickly as they emerge.
- **Model "yes behavior" yourself.** If you aren't willing to walk the yes walk, why should anyone else?

**The danger of situational tyrants:** Any organization, location, or department can become a breeding ground for *situational tyrants*—employees who have the power to say no within their tiny domains, and who exercise that power every chance they get. Avoid harboring and breeding such people, and keep a close eye and ear out throughout the organization to find out if, in spite of your best efforts, you have. (There is a parallel kind of tyranny to also guard against: the tyrannical treatment of *employees* by certain supervisors that is a problem in many organizations as well.)

*Note: I've compiled all of the reading group guides into a single document you can download for free at guides.micahsolomon.com.*

1. What are some examples of times when people in our organization have exhibited an attitude of "*The answer is 'yes!' Now what was your question?*" What about examples from other companies we have personally enjoyed doing business with?
2. As a rule, is "automatic positivity" happening right now in our organization—do we truly have a default of yes?
3. If not, or if not entirely, what are the roadblocks? Are they immovable or can they be shifted toward yes?
4. If the roadblocks don't seem immovable, would doing the work needed to create a default of yes be worth it? How so or how not?
5. On a more somber note, this chapter delves into the issue of "situational tyranny." Do we have our eyes out for this kind of behavior within our organization, both as it applies to the treatment of customers and as it applies to the treatment of employees, particularly when nobody powerful may be around to observe it?

**2**

# THE SECRETS OF BUILDING THE WORLD'S BEST CUSTOMER SERVICE CULTURE—YOURS

C ompany culture is currently a smoking-hot topic of business discussion, dilating a lot of pupils and inducing a lot of heavy breathing in the boardroom. Laying my own cards on the table, I can tell you that, in terms of feeding my family, this has been an excellent development: Culture has always been one of my favorite topics, and the opportunities to consult and speak on the subject have certainly been invigorating and welcome.

Yet there have been some odd, even bizarre, angles to the experience.

Out there working the "culture circuit," I've run into people whose ideas about culture change are comically distorted, kind of a mashup of

> "Let's hang some off-road bikes on the wall to illustrate
> our commitment to work-life balance!"
> —and—

"Maybe what we need are trendier-sounding job titles—'Ninja of the Backup Plan,' 'Goddess of the Interwebs,' 'Demigod of the Mailroom,' 'Queen of the Cloud'?"

—and—

"Hey, wouldn't a beer tap in the breakroom be a good idea? Or, hey, I've got it: Would a *vodka* tap be even better?"

I blame these dubious ideas about culture on the coverage the business press has given to successful companies that happen, *coincidental to their greatness,* to exhibit these types of flashy "cultural" elements. Although this sideshow gets all the attention, it's tangential to, or at odds with, the crux of what matters. (In the "at odds with" category: No, a beer or vodka tap in the break room is not a good idea. In fact, if you look in the Dictionary of Culture that I'm going to write someday, you'll find this under *N* for "No freakin' way is this a good idea.")

The essence of a strong customer service culture is simpler and more straightforward than you might think if you've let yourself get distracted by superficialities and hype. It is, in fact, relatively easy to understand and to get a start on implementing. It just takes the interest, a drive to succeed, and a little of what's (ironically) called common sense.

## Defining Customer Service Culture

My definition of *customer service culture*—the practical, working definition I use on the jobsite—is as simple as 1 and 2 (there's not even a 3). Your customer service culture, for better or for worse, has two primary elements:

1. The way your company treats its customers.
2. The way your company treats the people whose job it is to take care of these customers: employees, as well as vendors and subcontractors.

*The fundamental complication with this two-part definition is that there may not be an all-the-time way that you treat your customers or an all-the-time way that you treat employees, vendors, and subcontractors.* So, to get the full measure of a culture, we'll need to subdivide items 1 and 2 and look separately at:

- How you treat your customers, employees, vendors, and subcontractors on a normal, stress-free day (when money is flowing, nobody's called in sick, you've got your "A team" working [my Canadian clients call that their "eh team"]), and
- How you treat these entities when you are under stress (in the face of tight resources, hurricanes or other freakish weather on the horizon, demanding customers, intensive shareholder demands, difficult personal times for yourselves as employees and leaders, and so forth). In figure 2.1, *the goal is for the treatment in all four boxes to be equally positive.*

|  | When Stress Is Low ☀ | When Stress Is High ⛈ |
|---|---|---|
| **How We Serve Our Customers** | ? | ? |
| **How We Serve Those Who Serve Our Customers\*** | ? | ? |

\*Our employees, our vendors, and our subcontractors

Figure 2.1. The Solomon Service Culture Matrix™

For a printable copy, please email culture@micahsolomon.com

Unfortunately, some organizations differ dramatically in the treatment they offer in stressed versus unstressed scenarios. And it's here that cynicism can grow quickly: when customers and employees see you inconsistently deliver on your principles. (Just as bad, if a first-timer happens to catch your company on a bad [stressed] day, their *only* experience with you may be negative. In other words, they'll experience a defect rate of 100 percent!)

By contrast, when your culture is well-conceived and *consistently* implemented, an atmosphere settles in where service is *a way of life*, where it's *the standard position*, something that is continually lived, pursued, and refined. In such a culture, employees can perform practical magic that doesn't happen in lesser, internally conflicted organizations. In a positive service culture, employees are often to be found taking the initiative to care for their customers, and they're well known for how fair they are in their dealings with vendors and other stakeholders in every type of circumstance. Customers and other stakeholders learn over time that the company has their interests at heart regardless of whether skies are fair, threatening, or raining down buckets.

In a poorly conceived and inconsistent customer service culture, things will be askew in some or all of the following ways:

- The company will only *intermittently* uphold its commitment to providing good service (generally only doing so when times are low volume/low stress/ nobody's called in sick/the customer in question is a VIP, and so forth) rather than being a company that always does its very best for customers.
- The company will, at least some of the time, fail to support the people serving its customers—it will fail to empower employees, fail to give them creative leeway in how they go about their duties, and maybe even flat-out mistreat them.
- The company will, at least when times are tight, beat up vendors in brutal negotiations as well as openly devalue, even mock, their contributions.

You can get a hint of these out-of-whack scenarios when you see companies whose consumer reviews (such as on Yelp) and employee reviews (such as on Glassdoor) don't match up, with employees and customers having such disparate impressions that it seems as if they are describing entirely different companies. In a sense, they are.

## Five Steps Toward Creating a Customer Service Culture

Here are five steps to take toward establishing and sustaining a customer service culture:

1. Define your purpose in a sentence or two.
2. Set down a short list of principles that are fundamental to your desired culture.
3. Express your cultural expectations at every possible junction, from recruitment onward.
4. Maintain a repeating ritual for cultural reinforcement.
5. Develop an obsession with talent management.

**Define your purpose.** Write a sentence or two that defines the purpose of your business and describes the type of behaviors you'll be expecting from every associate, manager, and executive in your organization.

This statement of purpose should be:

- Written in clear language
- Short enough to be memorable
- Long enough to be meaningful

One of the most powerful definitions of purpose that I know of is the one that guides the Mayo Clinic:

**The needs of the patient come first.**

Mayo's statement is exceptionally brief (seven words), uses language that is easy to understand (the only word longer than one syllable is the central word, "patient"), and is clear in the expectations it lays out for everyone who works there.

Another powerful statement of purpose guides Safelite AutoGlass:

> **We exist to make a difference and bring unexpected happiness to people's everyday lives.**

The Safelite statement is only fourteen words long, and the only words that stray beyond two syllables are the salient ones: "unexpected," "difference," "happiness," and "everyday." Note in particular the "unexpected." Safelite associates tend to come into a customer's life on a day when happiness is the last thing they're expecting, yet the company devotes itself to the idea that its team will be able to bring happiness—unexpected happiness, in fact—in the course of their duties.

"You could think of us as being in the 'negative services' category," says Tom Feeney, Safelite's president and CEO. "Customers aren't in a good frame of mind after a rock hits their windshield, or, even worse, after someone breaks into their car, shattering the glass on the way in. So this is a very specific goal that we've embedded in our purpose statement, to 'bring unexpected happiness,' which suggests that we're going to wow customers even in the face of something that has them very frustrated."

Few definitions of purpose are *quite* as concise as these two, but concision and precision are exactly what you should be aiming for. It's essential to avoid the kind of flowery, jargon-infested statement whose inevitable fate will be to languish, unremembered, in somebody's desk drawer.

As you start to work on your organization's definition of purpose, it's certainly fine to *begin* by writing down something that's longer and more jargon-laden than you want to end up with. Just be sure to then whittle it down, taking out everything that is jargony, mealy-mouthed, or that you simply can't make yourself believe. Once you've done this, you'll have an expression of your culture's core purpose, defined in appropriately muscular and memorable language.

## THE NORDSTROM "DO-IT-NOW" SERVICE CULTURE

Joanne Hassis, the Nordstrom retail professional we first met on page 3, tells me she defines the Nordstrom culture as being a "do it now" culture, as long as the "it" is a pro-customer activity.

Here's an example I personally encountered of this "do it now, for the customer" culture.

When my Nordstrom shoe delivery was left in the rain by a common carrier (UPS or FedEx or DHL; I no longer remember) and my $200 shoes were ruined before they even got to me, it put things in a legal grey area. The responsible party *might* be me or it *might* be the trucking company, but to my understanding it's *not* Nordstrom.

Yet, when this happened to me, not for an instant did my salesperson, Joanne, even *consider* saying, "You need to file a claim with the trucking company."

Instead she told me, without hesitation, the following: "I'm so incredibly sorry that happened, and I'm bringing over a brand new pair of shoes—will you be home in forty-five minutes?"[I]

When I recently asked Joanne to tell me more about this "do it now" culture, she obliged. The Nordstrom culture "isn't something we spend much time defining or carrying on about," she told me. "Yet it is undeniably something you can feel in the air." A particularly inspiring aspect of the Nordstrom culture, she continued, is its circular nature: "The people who want to work here have been attracted by what they understand the Nordstrom culture to be. Then, once they get here, their enthusiasm drives all of us to live up to the best of what we can be—*to truly be as they believe us to be*." Finally, she says, the circle takes another fortuitous turn when *future* employees are attracted to the now-strengthened Nordstrom culture that has been created.

**Set down a short list of fundamental cultural principles, a sort of Constitution or Bill of Rights for what your culture will be.** I would suggest you limit yourself to no more than ten or twelve essential principles. Here are examples of what three such principles might look like:

- **We value every individual's input and creativity.** Everything we do here, from addressing defects to finding better ways to work, depends on employees' sharp eyes, input, and creativity. Every one of us here is valued for more than our labor, for more than what it says in our job descriptions.
- **We respond both to the stated requests of our customers and to opportunities to serve them in ways they may not directly request.** We can't always count on the customer to know what to ask for, nor to know what we are able to offer them.
- **Service is the responsibility of everyone here.** We seek out every opportunity to serve our customers and to improve their experiences, and we rise to the occasion to serve customers even when it pulls us away from our regularly assigned duties.

**Passionately express your cultural expectations at every possible juncture from recruitment, hiring, and employee onboarding onward.** Let employees and potential employees know, *from the first moment they come in contact with your organization,* what matters most in the culture you are striving to create. This is essential, and is often overlooked: recruiting, hiring, and onboarding so often get bogged down in forms to fill out and other mundane details that the new or potential employee never hears—or at least doesn't hear loud and clear—what the company they're joining, or are on the brink of joining, is all about.

**Introduce and diligently maintain a repeating ritual for cultural reinforcement.** Setting up the framework of a great service culture is only the start. *Reinforcing* it is what ultimately makes the difference. Time is your great enemy here or can be your dearest friend; time can either chip away, daily, at what you've built, through the relentless force of entropy, or time can be your dearest ally as you methodically reinforce and add texture and bulk to what you've built. Your best hope for having your service culture persist over time is to find an opportunity to reinforce your cultural focus every single day. Without this intentional daily rededication, the seed of cultural greatness that you're striving to plant may never take root, or may ultimately get washed away by competing goals and by the frustrations and challenges that employees endure each day in the course of serving customers.

One powerful ritual that works in many types of organizations is what I call a daily **Customer Service Minute**. (In spite of its name, it will more likely require five minutes, but keep it under ten.) Hold your Customer Service Minute at the beginning of each workday (or at the beginning of each shift, if you run more than one shift a day). Some of my consulting clients call this their "huddle," or "lineup," or "standup meeting" (I'm not a fan of this last, disability-insensitive term); whatever you decide to call it, it will be a ritual that involves employees—ideally, *all* employees—who gather in small groups at the same time each day to kick off the workday, or shift, on the right note.

Each Customer Service Minute should be devoted to a single aspect of providing great service. This typically includes sharing examples that illustrate that single service principle as well as going over helpful techniques, pitfalls encountered, and challenges overcome. I recommend that the Customer Service Minute be led by a *different* employee (not necessarily a manager, by the way) each day; if you take this approach, your employees, in rotation, will be learning and teaching at the same time, and you'll avoid overburdening any manager or single team member.

(Not exactly a repeating *ritual*, but having similar utility, is printed collateral—as long as it's well thought out and you keep it up to date. Ritz-Carlton Hotel Company employees swear by the value of the pocket-sized accordion card of key principles and behavioral guidance that they keep on their person and can refer to in the course of their workday; Jason Bradshaw and team at Volkswagen Australia have had similar success keeping their dealers inspired through their brief, illustrated book, designed for internal use only: *100 Ways to WOW.*)

**Develop an obsession with talent management.** Talent management is the term I use for the recruitment, selection, and development of employees. As much as anywhere, this is where culture lives or dies. It's essential that you implement a successful approach and mindset for finding, keeping, and developing employees who have an affinity for service: employees who are selected for their interest in and suitability for your company purpose and whom you support and guide in their further development. (Talent management is one of the central disciplines of cultural and professional success when serving customers. There's a longer treatment of it in chapter 3.)

## RESOURCES FOR READERS

If you'd like additional help in creating and sustaining a customer service culture, I have a printable document that can help. For a copy of "Eleven Powerful Customer Service Culture Catalysts (That Can Transform Your Company Results)," let me know by email at culturelist@micahsolomon.com (careful—my URL is very error-inducing) and I'll hook you up.

## Ten Elements Shared by
## Outstanding Customer Service Cultures

In the time I've spent studying, and working with, companies with truly outstanding customer service cultures (such as Nordstrom, USAA, Southwest Airlines, The Container Store, Zappos, L.L. Bean, Mayo Clinic, MOD Pizza, and Bob's Red Mill) and these companies' equally excellent but lesser-known business-to-business (B2B) counterparts, I find each company's culture to be, on the surface, quite distinct. For example, an employee whose early career is spent in the straitlaced but excellent Member Support environment of USAA in San Antonio and then moves to Vegas to join the wild-and-woolly world of the Customer Loyalty Team at Zappos is *definitely* going to need an adjustment period before feeling at home. Yet, just below the surface distinctions, these cultures have a lot in common.

I've gone ahead and distilled a list of ten characteristics that I believe to be shared by all great customer service cultures. I recommend reviewing this list and considering how your *own* company culture stacks up. Then, wherever you find yourself lacking, get ready to roll up your sleeves.

1. **Culturally consonant employee selection (hiring) practices.** Sustaining a great customer service culture is much more possible if employees have a natural predisposition to serve. While there's no complete guarantee that every employee hired via a trait-based selection approach (which I will discuss in the next chapter) will fulfill their potential and advance the company culture, great companies understand that this is the right place to start.

2. **A commitment to ongoing improvement via customer service training and retraining, from orientation**

(onboarding) onward. Training can take many shapes, from the initial inspiration and guidance that new employees receive at the time of orientation, to the Customer Service Minute, to more elaborate training sessions, workshops, and all-hands keynotes with a customer service theme. All of these are ways that great customer service cultures maintain themselves and ensure that they continue to grow. This way, service greatness isn't left to happenstance and doesn't plateau or diminish over time from inertia and entropy.

3. **A culture of empowering *every* employee to take the initiative in service of their customers.** Once employees are properly selected, oriented, and trained, they require empowerment to flourish. All of these primed-to-be-great employees can't do their best work, or contribute to the greatness of a service culture, until they're given the power and leeway to do so. And all great customer service cultures *do* give employees such power and leeway. In fact, it's understood, in a service culture such as predominates at Nordstrom or Zappos or the Ritz-Carlton Hotel Company, that as an employee it's *your job* to be empowered: to take positive, creative action on behalf of others.

4. **Employee control over how they carry out their duties.** In a great company culture, not only are employees empowered to assist customers in proactive (and, at times, inconvenient or expensive) ways, they also have a level of creative control over how they carry out their day-to-day duties. Although great companies provide comprehensive guidance and training, they don't excessively script or regiment employees in how to carry out their interactions with customers. Employees are not, in other words, just interchangeable cogs, nor are they serfs to be exploited solely for

their labor. They are fully dimensional human beings who are both expected to and supported in making full and unique contributions.

5. **A common language.** At Zappos, employees refer to themselves as Zapponians; their lobby gift shop is the Z'Boutique, the contact center is called the Customer Loyalty Team, and so forth. Southwest Airlines creatively spells words such as "luv" in its mission statement and internal documents. This kind of common language, though it may seem goofy to outsiders, is useful in bringing a company together and making everyone who works at a company feel like they're part of the "in crowd." (Be careful here: internal jargon shouldn't be allowed to slip into conversation or correspondence with *customers*, as it will likely confuse them or make them feel like outsiders.)

6. **Legendary stories.** Tales of over-the-top customer service are valuable in making a point to prospective, incoming, and even long-tenured employees about what an organization's culture consists of and what it places a value on. Southwest Airlines has many such stories, often about assisting passengers in distress; similarly, USAA Insurance has many inspiring tales that get told internally, often stemming from work they've done for their members in flood recovery and other disaster assistance. Each such story serves the same purpose: to show what is valued in the company's culture and the lengths to which employees should be willing to go in terms of investing empathy, resources, and creativity.

7. **No "not my job."** There's an understanding within great company cultures that every employee will pitch in wherever needed, regardless of an employee's particular job description and level in the organization. This can manifest itself daily, as it does at Disney

parks, where employees ("cast members") from each and every level of the organization can be found interrupting whatever else they may be doing to pick up stray trash wherever they encounter it. Or this pitching in outside of an employee's daily functions can come up primarily on special occasions, the days or peak hours when help is needed to handle additional volume. For example, during the holiday rush, every Zappos employee, including CEO Tony Hsieh and other members of the executive team, spends time working the phone lines shoulder-to-shoulder with the regular call center employees. Similarly, at the Ritz-Carlton Hotel Company, when there's a time-sensitive need to convert a meeting room setup into a banquet room arrangement or vice versa, it's "all hands on deck" until accomplished.

8. **Pride.** At Southwest Airlines, which is frequently rated at or near the top within aviation for customer service, employee pride is palpable. Case in point: Once, when I told a flight attendant what I do for a living, she asked for my address and mailed me *her own copy* of *Nuts!*, a classic book about Southwest. Inside, scribbled throughout the book, were forty or so of her own notes, comments like, "So true! We really *do* try to do this for our passengers," and "Yes! This is *exactly* how we aim to treat each other!" and "This is what makes working here amazing!" Again: This was not a publicist trying to gain an advantage with me. This was a flight attendant promoting her own company on her own initiative, and at her own expense.

9. **Humility.** The same companies that exhibit such pride are also, paradoxically, humble in ways that keep an organization both solidly rooted and open to learning and growth. Case in point: In response

to my articles covering Nordstrom's customer service prowess, people from a variety of levels of the Nordstrom organization have written to me and posted various comments. What's notable to me about these comments is how uniformly they include an element of humility and eagerness to improve, rather than patting themselves on the back for the positive coverage I've provided in the published piece. These responses fall essentially along the lines of, "Thanks for the recognition in your article. We're just striving to provide the best service we can and to improve every day."

10. **Support for customer-focused innovation.** A great customer service culture can't be static. Happily, employees within a positive culture, simply due to their pro-customer inclinations, will find multiple areas for improvement, each and every shift they work. While this, of course, is a great start, it's ultimately not enough. Customer-focused innovation thrives when a progressive attitude is supported by processes and systems to harvest employee ideas and bring them to fruition. (*Please see the USAA sidebar immediately below for more on this subject. You may also enjoy a document I have available to support innovation in your organization. For a free copy of "25 Essential Innovation Prompts," email me at* **innovation@micahsolomon.com**.)

## HOW USAA BAKES CUSTOMER EXPERIENCE INNOVATION INTO ITS COMPANY CULTURE

Here's a jaw-dropping illustration of what a culture that's focused on customer experience innovation looks like: the ideas proposed by *a single security guard* working at USAA, the insurance and financial services giant, have resulted in *twenty-five patents* for the company. These patents, each designed to improve a portion of the customer experience provided to USAA customers ("members" in USAA parlance) are just a few of the 10,000 ideas submitted by employees each year, with over 900 suggestions resulting in US patents so far.

How does USAA, which regularly ranks at or near the top for customer satisfaction in all of its markets, propel customer-focused innovation? There are some clever processes involved, and I'll get to those in a moment. But what it requires, first off, is a mindset.

"You have to realize," says Darrius Jones, vice president for innovation, "that every employee here is a customer—a member—of USAA. You get your membership with your initial onboarding documents. [USAA membership is otherwise restricted to current and retired military and their families.] This, combined with serving members every day, keeps employees in constant touch with how USAA does business" and keeps them acutely aware of ways that USAA could potentially improve its service to members, including themselves.

## INNOVATION COMES TO THE AID OF HURRICANE-FLOODED CUSTOMERS

Some innovations proposed by USAA employees come in response to heart-wrenching developments experienced by an employee either in their own life or encounters in the course of helping out customers. That's the genesis of the aerial imaging tool that was developed in the wake of Hurricane Harvey: "Our claims adjusters heard from members who couldn't get home and were desperate to see what damage would be awaiting them," Lea Sims, USAA's assistant vice president for employee and member innovation, tells me. "Within twenty-four hours, several teams here working together constructed an online portal with 'before' and 'after' aerial photos using existing satellite imagery and post-storm imagery from NOAA (National Oceanic and Atmospheric Administration) to determine the extent of damages. This gave our members the ability to remotely search and view damage to their homes during the hurricane, which helped them begin the rebuilding process before they had a chance to physically get back to their homes."

## GETTING CLOSE TO THE CUSTOMER—IN THIS CASE, DEPLOYED MILITARY AND THEIR FAMILIES

In addition to innovations that arise from employees' own experiences as USAA members, there are those that come out of employees' understanding of the experience of USAA's broader member base, in particular, deployed military and their families. Every new USAA employee goes through an onboarding experience for military-life awareness that includes preparing and eating MREs (meals ready to eat) and drilling with a retired drill sergeant. (I understand that he takes it somewhat easier on them than he does on real troops!)

How this plays out on the banking side is instructive. USAA's banking operation is, for the most part, branchless, in the belief that phone- and digitally based experiences are most appropriate for a far-flung membership. Being largely branchless and serving a unique population led USAA to become the first major US financial institution to roll out voice and facial recognition, technological innovations based in part on an employee contribution that was ultimately awarded a patent.

## HARVESTING AND REWARDING INNOVATIVE IDEAS

The systems USAA has set up to harvest innovative ideas include its "Always On Ideas Platform," a portal that's available to all employees, as well as what USAA calls challenges, competitions, and hackathons. "Challenges are where business sponsors within USAA present a problem or challenge and ask employee innovators to provide ideas for solving it," says Sims. "Competitions are volunteer-based and more involved, taking about eight weeks to complete with sessions over lunches. Hackathons are sponsored by particular departments within USAA and are designed to be rapid-fire problem solving over a day or two."

The rewards? While employee ideas (considered "work product") do remain the property of USAA, the company does provide recognition and rewards, including monetary rewards for winners of hackathons and competitions as well as recognition at innovation ceremonies, and, for those whose inventions are awarded a patent, the immortality of being featured on a leaf of the Patent Tree, which has grown to take up an entire wall of the company's innovation lab.

## Serving the People Who Serve Your Customers

Nothing boils my blood quicker than a company leader who shows superficial interest in my service culture matrix (see page 15) yet manages to pass over the "how we serve those who serve our customers" row as if it somehow doesn't apply to them. *Great* companies and *great* leaders don't do this. Rather, they strive to give both columns in the matrix—*serving customers* and *serving those who serve our customers*—equal, or nearly equal, weight.

But rather than go on ranting about the culturally hypocritical corners of the business world, let me highlight two companies that walk the walk: independent insurance company Starkweather and Shepley and the fast-growing casual restaurant chain MOD Pizza.

If the insurance industry doesn't sound like a hotbed of cultural leadership to you, that might be because you've yet to come across a company like Starkweather. The sustained growth of this firm, one of the top independent insurance agencies overall in New England and one of the largest independent agencies nationwide for the personal insurance sector, is based on the systemic, culture-building decisions that the 140-year-old company has made over the course of many decades.

Strikingly, their employee focus is built into their company charter, and it forms an essential part of who they are. Uniquely, Starkweather is an insurance company that's held in trust for the benefit of its employees, and with a stated commitment that the firm will never be sold. "The intentions and interests of the trust are not based on returns to shareholder stock," says Chairman and CEO Larry Keefe. "Instead, the trust structure ensures the firm's existence in perpetuity for the benefit of our clients and our associates." This is a rare position and structure in an industry environment that's so rife with consolidation that employees elsewhere in the industry are commonly fearful that they'll come into work one morning and find an entirely different corporate parent in charge.

"Operating for the sake of our stakeholders [employees] and our clients is woven into the structure of how we do business here," says executive vice president and national sales manager Andy Fotopulos. "I used to go to annual meetings [at previous companies], and the person on the podium would be up there talking about 'making decisions that are best for clients,' or 'making decisions that are best for employees.' The sad truth, though, is that while many companies talk this talk, it wasn't 'til I got to Starkweather that I had the beautiful 'aha!' moment: 'My gosh, here it is absolutely true.' Every decision we make is what's best for our employees and our clients—and they are considered hand in hand."

## MOD Pizza: Second Chances for Employees; First-Class Service for Customers

Maybe a quick-service pizza chain seems like another unlikely place to uncover a superior service culture, but I'd beg to differ, having spent time with MOD Pizza, the chain of pizza restaurants that is spreading across North America like a river of melted mozzarella. MOD is already operating more than 400 restaurants (a figure I've had to revise five times in the course of writing this book, they're growing so quickly), after only ten years in business.

But growth isn't thought of at MOD as the goal. Rather, it's considered an *aftereffect* of MOD's central purpose, which I would distill down to three words: *"Putting People First."*

"Putting People First" is pursued with great passion by management and employees companywide, who are empowered to make special efforts to hire "second chance" employees (former prisoners and people who have suffered from addiction) and those with special physical and intellectual needs, as well as making other accommodations that fall under the umbrella of putting people first. "It is our feeling and our strategy," says Ally Svenson, who cofounded the company with her husband Scott in 2008, "that the employees we treat so well" after their years of bad breaks previously, "will have an innate passion to serve. In some cases, MOD means even more to our employees than it does to Scott and me, and because of its importance in their lives, our employees have a passion that comes out in how they serve their customers in every interaction, day after day."

# READER'S CHEATSHEET FOR CHAPTER 2

My definition of *customer service culture* has two primary elements:

1. The way your company treats its customers.
2. The way your company treats the people whose job it is to take care of these customers: your employees, vendors, and subcontractors.

To make it trickier, we need to subdivide items 1 and 2 between how you treat your customers, employees, vendors, and subcontractors on a normal, stress-free day and how you treat them when your organization is under stress. In an ideal organization, the difference will be minimized between the behaviors you'll find on display at stressed and unstressed times and times when it's serving external customers versus when it's serving those *who take care* of customers (see the matrix illustration on page 15).

## Five Steps Toward Creating a Customer Service Culture

Here are five essential steps for establishing and sustaining a customer service culture:

1. **Define your purpose** in a sentence or two.
2. **Write down a brief list of fundamental cultural principles**—sort of a Constitution or Bill of Rights for what your culture will be.
3. **Express your cultural expectations (items 1 and 2 above) during recruitment, hiring, and onboarding**—so that they are known to employees and potential employees from the get-go.
4. **Introduce and maintain a repeating ritual for cultural reinforcement** such as a **Customer Service Minute:** a very brief meeting (shorter than ten minutes) at the beginning of each workday, or the beginning of each shift, if you run more than one shift a day. Focus each of these sessions on a single aspect of providing great service.
5. **Become organizationally obsessed with talent management.** Devote yourself to finding, keeping, and developing employees who have an affinity for service, whom you then support and guide in further developing their cultural affinity.

## Ten Elements That Great Customer Service Cultures Share

1. Culturally consonant employee selection (hiring) practices.
2. Customer service training and retraining, from orientation (onboarding) onward.
3. Employee empowerment to serve customers creatively and to the best of their abilities.
4. Significant employee control over how to carry out their jobs.
5. A common language.
6. Legendary stories.
7. No "not my job."
8. Pride in the company and its place in the world.
9. Humility about the company and its place in the world.
10. Support for customer-focused innovation.

1. One point that's emphasized in this chapter is that a great customer service culture treats those who serve customers (employees, vendors, subcontractors) every bit as well as it treats the customers themselves. To what extent is our own organization succeeding—or failing to uphold this standard?

2. Just as important, a great customer culture strives to treat customers and employees just as well during times when the organization is *under stress* (when resources are tight, the weather is threatening, customers are introducing challenges in the workflow, and so forth) *as it does in times of ease* (when money is flowing, nobody's called in sick, the sun is shining, and the phone queues are short). To what extent is our attitude and our behaviors uniform regardless of whether our organization is under stress?

3. This chapter includes a list of ten elements that Micah has found that all great customer service cultures share (culturally consonant employee selection practices; customer service training and retraining; employee empowerment; creative control that is entrusted to employees; a common language; legendary stories; no "not my job"; pride; humility; and support for customer-focused innovation). Do we agree with this

list? If so, does it match what's going on at our organization pretty well, sort of, or absolutely not?

Reminder: All of the reading group guides are available as a single document you can download for free at **guides.micahsolomon.com**.

# 3

# TALENT MANAGEMENT: RECRUITING, SELECTING, AND NURTURING THE TEAM WHO WILL POWER YOUR SUCCESS

Talent management—how you recruit, select, and nurture employees—is, perhaps more than any other discipline, the foundation of your company's ability to create and sustain a superior customer experience.

Succeeding in talent management isn't a simple proposition. There's a lot to get right and plenty of opportunities to get tripped up. While a single chapter isn't nearly enough to cover everything that needs to be said on the subject (and it would be insulting to the fabulous professionals who work in this discipline to suggest otherwise), I'm going to use these pages to share the essence of my philosophy and some practical pointers intended to get you going in the right direction.

## The Promise of Trait-Based Hiring

When you're selecting new employees for roles where they'll be interacting with customers (and, likewise, when you're moving existing employees into such roles), the approach that, by and large, works best is to give more weight to personality traits than to previously acquired skills and experience.

This is because the technical, vocational aspects of most positions can be taught to nearly any employee, but personality traits *tend to* have calcified by the time an applicant reaches adulthood.* If you bring on new employees who lack the right personality traits for service, even if they are otherwise qualified, you're going to find them struggling in their roles every step of the way, and it's going to be a struggle in which their best efforts—and yours—may never emerge victorious.

It's at best an uphill battle, and at worst an impossibility, to try to *make* people enjoy other people, *make* them empathetic, or *make* them enjoy being part of a team working together on behalf of customers. Danny Meyer, the acclaimed New York restaurateur, explains his thinking when it comes to hiring: "If you have the right hospitality quotient" (the emotional traits that Meyer finds essential for succeeding in service) "but lack technical knowledge, that doesn't worry us. We think we can do a pretty effective job at helping you to improve technically. We're concerned, on the other hand, about hiring anyone without those emotional skills, because those are pretty much baked into people by the time we meet them—and are a lot less teachable."

## How to Find the Right People, and How to Stop Finding the Wrong Ones

Before I spell out how to determine which prospective employees have the right traits for customer-facing roles, I need to cure you of the *wrong* way of going about it: going with your gut. Your gut—your

---

* I don't want to overstate this; there absolutely are exceptions, some of them wonderful and dramatic!

instinct for picking the future superstars of customer service—is probably not as spot-on as you think it is. Just as most every driver on the road believes their own driving skills to be above average, a lot of managers and leaders in the world of business believe themselves to have an above-average ability to spot future high-performing employees. But, as the carnage on our roads and the multitudes of inappropriately selected employees can attest, not every driver, and not every manager, can be above average. *

This common yet unwarranted cockiness is due to a psychological phenomenon called the *self-serving bias*. This bias causes us to *attribute whatever successes we have to our talents* and to *ascribe any failures to external events and bad luck*. The self-serving bias (as it applies to hiring decisions) deludes us into thinking we have a special gift for employee selection by giving ourselves credit for the times when we just got lucky and, when we were wrong, letting us off the hook by rationalizing such failures as flukes.

Instead of going with your gut, a better approach is to bring *science* into the employee-selection process, with the goal of eliminating as much happenstance as possible. Generally, I suggest you do this by engaging the services of one of the companies that specialize in this discipline, such as Predictive Index, HUMANeX, Gallup, and Talent Plus.

However, if you can't afford to hire a full-service employee selection partner such as one of these, it may be possible to put together a somewhat similar approach on your own, at least if you run a small (or smallish) business.

*(An essential caveat before we go any further: There are essential EEOC-enforceable practices that you need to follow in relation to screening and selection that I am unable to cover here. Two of these principles, in very broad strokes, are to apply any screening equitably across all applicants and to ensure that the actual screening itself is equitable in nature; but*

---

* Please be sure to see the Diversity and Inclusion Notes at the end of this chapter for an important additional discussion along these lines.

*even those two principles don't come close to covering everything that needs to be covered. Addressing these issues is both essential and beyond the scope of the insights I am able to offer you here.)*

To take this more DIY approach, you would license a less comprehensive (and therefore less expensive) off-the-shelf diagnostic profiling tool that purports to be able to screen for the characteristics necessary for customer-facing work. Then, you'd *broadly* verify the applicability of your new profiling tool as follows: ask a few of your best employees to go through the profiling, and also have a few of your solid-but-less-dramatically-distinguished employees to do the same. (I'm counting on you to have the good sense to not phrase your invitation as, "Hey, not particularly distinguished employee, would you mind helping me out with this project?")

What you're trying to find out is this: *Can the profiling tool that you've licensed distinguish between these two categories of employees?* Do your existing, outstanding employees also look outstanding *on paper*? And are your middle-of-the-road employees' scores appropriately middle of the road? If so, you can have some confidence that you've *roughly* verified this profiling tool's validity.

You may also want to augment your profiling instrument with some commonsense approaches:

- **Use behavioral-based interviewing.** I have a lot of skepticism about traditional job interviews; there is data that, unfortunately, suggests that employment interviews are best at showing who is good at being interviewed rather than who will be good at doing the job once hired. But if you are going to base hiring decisions in whole or in part on interviews, be sure to include a lot of "Tell me about a time that you did *X*" type of questions and go easy on the "What are your strengths and weaknesses?" questions. You'll get a fuller picture of your applicant this way.

■ **Pay attention to how the applicant treats your existing employees.** Ann Alba, the resident manager of the triple-Five Star, double-Five Diamond Broadmoor Hotel in Colorado Springs, Colorado (that's fifteen stars from *Forbes* and ten diamonds—the maximum possible—from AAA)—says that she has learned more about applicants from how they treat her employees than she has by conducting formal interviews. "I believe almost anyone can build themselves up for a good interview," she says. "I'm more interested in what I hear back from my team about how [the prospect] treated the garage attendant as they arrived on the property; how they treated the receptionist; how they interacted with the staff they passed in the hall; because *that* shows the true customer service heart and how real it is." Danny Meyer agrees, and has top applicants visit with his team, shadowing them as they perform their duties, before they're made permanent with the company. After the shadowing is complete, Meyer looks for feedback from team members at all levels of the organization who encountered the applicant in this nearly real-life situation.[1]

## Don't Send in the Clones

I don't want to accidently lead you into thinking that, by getting scientific about hiring, your goal should be to end up with a homogenous, clonelike group of employees. *Your goal should be pretty much the opposite.* The idea of selecting based on traits is that *it should open you up to a wider group of potential employees than you might otherwise consider.* Trait-based hiring is designed to discover what lies underneath, to uncover the potential customer service superstars who don't interview well or who are different age-wise, gender-wise, in appearance, in physical abilities, or in personal background from what your mind may have unconsciously typecast for their roles.

## Casting a Wide Net

Even if you're rigorous in selecting the best prospects from your applicant pool, it's hard to get great results when you're choosing employees from a pool of applicants that's too small. If this is the case, you may find yourself forced to settle for, say, 40 percent of the applications you receive. These aren't attractive odds; it's unlikely that a full 40 percent of *any* group of applicants are aligned with what's needed to give great service. Your results will improve if you invest in sufficient outreach to allow you to restrict yourself to hiring only the top 10 percent or even the top 1 percent of applicants—the best of the best.

"The secret is ABS: Always Be Scouting," says Brad Black, president and CEO of HUMANeX, a company that assists service-focused organizations with their hiring: You should be recruiting, or at least screening, prospective employees 24 hours a day, he says, via what Black calls "a marriage of technology and science."

Recruiting 24/7 works like this: Offer a set of preliminary questions in a format that can be accessed remotely and around the clock. Applicants who make it through this initial screening can be automatically invited at the end of the screening to sign up for step two of the process, which will be a telephone interview. This way, an applicant who is working two jobs at present and can only find time to apply at, say, 11:00 p.m., can, if they make it through the screening, receive serious, sincere interest from your company that very same night in the form of an invitation to take the next step toward coming to work for you.

If you embrace this approach of screening 24/7 and are diligent about getting back to prospects in a timely manner, you'll soon find yourself able to select employees from a larger and more varied pool than if you only recruit when it's convenient for *you*, rather than for those who may want to apply. And this can make all the difference.

## "HIRE SLOWLY, FIRE QUICKLY" IS JUST AN EVIL SOUNDBITE

"Hire slowly, fire quickly" is a soundbite you've probably heard a lot in the business press (though generally *not* from human resources (HR) professionals, by the way). Though this concept is 50 percent along the lines of what I'm spelling out in this chapter—the "hire slowly" (or at least carefully) part—it's the other 50 percent that troubles me. "Fire quickly," applied to those who don't immediately thrive in your organization, means throwing away human potential in a way that is unnecessary and cruel: a blip on a résumé for the employee and wasted resources for your company, not to mention the shockwaves felt by those in your organization who are left, for now, unfired.

In my experience, great companies engage in the more difficult "coach quickly," "make adjustments quickly," and "amp up the training 'til they succeed," rather than the knee jerkish (and plain old jerkish) "fire quickly."

## Unlocking Employees' Voluntary Efforts

Exceptional customer service requires more than selecting the right employees. It requires convincing those employees to contribute their extra, optional, discretionary efforts—the stuff that's not specifically spelled out in their job description—and *that they can choose to either withhold from or contribute to your organization*.

The tricky thing about highly capable employees is that their aptitude can allow them to coast if they're uninspired.

Presumably, though, you didn't hire these wonderfully high-potential employees in order to then watch them deliver a mere baseline performance. You hired them for the *extra* something they can bring to your organization. And unless you make an effort to tease this out of them, you probably aren't going to get it.

So, how do you get that extra something out of a new employee's performance? A good start is to make sure your employees *know, from the get-go, what you want from them.* Once employees understand what you really want—your aspirations for your organization and for employees who work there—most of them are going to do their best to give it to you.

## Focus Your Onboarding on Purpose

The best time to make this happen is right away: during orientation (or "onboarding"), a crucial time in an organization's relationship with a new employee. Employees are particularly impressionable during their first days on the job. In this time of upheaval, they're looking for something to hold onto, ideally something positive. So, don't squander this powerful moment by wasting it on minutiae and technicalities. Instead, use this opportunity to tell new employees about your vision, about their purpose as employees in your organization, about what truly matters in providing superior customer service. Get this across now, in clear and memorable terms, and save the nitty-gritty details for later. And, ideally, if you want to make these essential points stick, have a person from high up in your leadership—even, as is the case in some extraordinary organizations, the CEO—personally get these points across about values, beliefs, and purpose. It's *that* kind of important. Employees will only be new once.

## Talent Management and Employee Growth

Even after you've selected the right employee and welcomed them with an orientation that communicates your organizational purpose, this perfectly selected, newly arrived employee is still only a seed of what's to come. Lack of light and water can kill that seed pretty quickly or can cause that seed (stick with me here as I mutilate the metaphor!) to wander over to more fertile ground at a different company. "You need to be developing your new employees, coaching them, immersing them in a culture that allows the building of great teams," explains Brad Black. If not, you'll experience low engagement and high turnover—negative results that affect the customer experience, the morale of remaining employees, and organizational effectiveness overall.

A key here is to be *systematic* in the development of employees throughout their tenure. Managers should hold discussions with each employee at set intervals (ninety days can be ideal) to ensure that employees are progressing in relation to their potential and their desires for career growth. At these meetings, as well as at a longer and more involved annual check-in, managers should be asking about the time that has passed and where the employees see themselves in the future, as well as giving employees feedback about their talents, as measured empirically and objectively, so that, as Black puts it, "whatever the employees' talents are, you're helping them to grow."

## Employees Deserve Input into How Their Duties Are Designed and Carried Out

There's one final talent management imperative that I want to convey: *employees deserve to have input into the design of their work*. Employee and employer alike benefit from this latitude: it stimulates employee development, leads to happier, more fulfilled employees, and allows a company to glean input and insights that the employees would be withholding otherwise.

To be flexible in this manner as an employer requires resisting an archaic strain of business thinking left over from the Industrial Revolution: the mindset that employees are mere cogs in a machine, hired to perform tasks without variation, in a precise manner that has been laid out by their (so-called)[2] superiors. Here's the approach you need instead: accept that even though you may need to let your employees know *what* they need to get done (what the objectives of the company are and how their position in the company fits into these), you avoid, where practical, dictating *how* they should go about designing their day and carrying out their duties.

If employees are only doing what they do because you've spelled out every little detail for them, you haven't created a sustainable approach to customer service excellence. The daily delivery of service excellence is powered and sustained by employees who are allowed and encouraged to be, in a meaningful way, part of the uniqueness of that delivery.

## HOW TO THINK ABOUT DIFFERENT GENERATIONS IN THE WORKPLACE—AND GET THE MOST OUT OF THE RAPIDLY EXPANDING MILLENNIAL COMPONENT

As you strive to succeed in talent management, one trap that lies in wait for you is the fallacy that everyone in a generation acts like everyone else in that generation, and that it's possible, therefore, to "generationally manage" your workforce. This so radically overstates the difference between generations that it fails, almost wholly, to be a useful way to think of the people who work for you.

Here's an alternative, more nuanced, view of your workforce: Although there are, *on average*, differences between generations, these are dwarfed by the sharper distinctions you'll find between individual human beings, even those of similar ages. And *individual human beings, rather than generations, are what make up a workforce.*

In particular, regarding your millennial employees, I take exception to the vocal chorus that's been ranting about "kids these days"—young employees who, so the prejudiced and prejudicial talk goes, "expect medals for just showing up." Not only am I not interested in piling on, I don't think "kids these days" are deserving of any such pile-on. Millennial employees represent the best-educated (they have the most education, and many have been taught computer programming and other advanced skills as early as middle school) and most thoughtfully raised (more about that below) cohort in history. And even if you disagree with this assessment, you'd best get used to these younger workers. It's predicted that by 2025, three-quarters of all workers globally will be millennials.[3]

Having said this, it's true that the members of different generations tend to bring, *on average*, different expectations to the workplace and that there's value in understanding what these expectations are and fulfilling them to the best of your ability as an employer. As far as millennials are concerned, here are some common employee expectations, coupled with suggestions for how to address them:

**I. They're hungry for feedback, so give it to them.** Many millennials have experienced close involvement from parents, teachers, and mentors throughout their education, which means that they've grown accustomed to receiving extensive performance feedback from adults. This can lead to a jarring contrast for them when they arrive at their first professional position and suddenly can't find anyone who's interested in telling them how they're doing.

One millennial told me, poignantly, about his experience at his first job: "This was the first time in my life that nobody cared about the quality of my work—or if they did care, I couldn't tell. I could be doing great work, or work that was just okay; the response I received was the same either way."

The solution here is obvious, and it provides an organizational win regardless of generation: *provide more input.* Not just via formal, periodic performance reviews, but through informal responses offered daily or weekly. Your employees will appreciate this, and you'll be helping them contribute the best of what they have to offer.

**2. They want to share responsibility—so find ways to let them.** In many cases, millennials were raised by parents whose style of parenting supported individual empowerment, often including children in family decision-making from an early age. *

Now, as millennial employees enter the early stages of their careers, they look for work to take them beyond a feeling of powerlessness as part of a massive machine. Because of this, as Jay Coldren, a noted service professional currently serving as a managing director at Streetsense, puts it, "There's value in trying to create opportunities that give millennial employees the chance to take responsibility and find success on a micro level before they move on to larger roles."

Millennials have a tendency to expect career advancement on a time-table that may strike their managers as unrealistic. As one executive told me, "Great [young] people are coming into our industry who are highly educated and who all want to be directors of everything immediately." The most successful response to this is a simple one: *compromise*. Make it clear that advancement isn't possible on the millennial's idealized schedule, but that if they make a commitment to their current position and department that may seem lengthy to them—yet is shorter than the current norm in your company—they will be rewarded with additional opportunities for growth on a timetable they can depend on.

---

* A *very* early age. At age three, my millennial daughter had already figured out how to adapt—I don't want to say "twist"—our collaborative style of language to the purpose of wielding influence over her doting parents. Once, as my wife and I were discussing which white-tablecloth restaurant we should go to for dinner, we heard her tiny toddler's voice chime in from the back seat of the car, "I think we should all *compromise* and go to McDonald's."

**3. Support their desire for work-life balance.** Members of the millennial generation are often unwilling to sacrifice their off-hours or make other lifestyle compromises in return for financial compensation. There have been various theories about the reason millennials tend to value work-life balance so strongly, but regardless of the origins of this stance, it needs to be taken into consideration by employers today.

There's no silver bullet solution here that I'm aware of. Humane scheduling is an issue that has stumped even companies with otherwise-positive employee relations. A start is to accept that this generation's desire for work-life balance is a *positive* goal and that any scheduling solutions that achieve it will also benefit your overall workforce. *The desire to have a life outside of work is not exclusive to any one generation.*

**4. Let them work for an ethical organization—by being one.** Millennials tend to be concerned about organizational ethics and social responsibility, often referred to as CSR: corporate social responsibility. If you can satisfy these concerns, it will go a long way toward helping you recruit and retain your pick of employees.

CSR concerns often relate to the creation of the product or service you sell: the ethics of your supply chain. This is an area where high standards, transparency, and avoiding the temptation to "greenwash" (make false or overstated environmental claims) or "causewash" (make inaccurate claims relating to other aspects of social responsibility, such as labor practices) are essential.

Closer to home, employees and potential employees will also pay attention to the ethics of life around the office, a subject that, more than supply chain considerations, is directly in their faces.

Even *literally* in their faces! One way that some particularly peachy employers succeed in enticing and retaining ethics-minded employees, including millennials, is one of the most elemental: through attention to what's available for employees to put in their mouths and stomachs. If you were to write down a list of some of the most attractive employers out there—Google, Oracle, LinkedIn, Twitter—you would also be looking at the client list of Bon Appétit Management, the company that runs these organizations' employee cafes while maintaining the ethical stances and behaviors that employees demand. Bon Appétit was one of the first signatories—way back in 2002—to the Seafood Watch sustainability guidelines; it's been involved with farmworkers' rights since the company's inception; and it's been tackling the issue of food's relationship to climate change as well. "Great companies want great employees, and great employees want to feel *well*-fed and *ethically* fed at work. That's where we come in," says Cary Wheeland, a senior vice president at Bon Appétit. "Particularly in today's market, this has become a significant hiring and retention tool for our corporate clients."

*Note: This discussion has exclusively covered millennials as <u>employees</u>. For a look at millennials as <u>customers</u>, see the sidebar in chapter 5.*

*"GET TO THE POINT,*

*MICAH!"*

# READER'S CHEATSHEET
# FOR CHAPTER 3

**Talent management:** The way you recruit, select, and nurture the people who serve your customers, is one of the most essential keys to succeeding with customer service.

**Trait-based hiring:** When recruiting new employees, consider using a trait-based approach, because if you hire a prospect for employment who lacks the right *traits* for customer-facing work, they're likely to find themselves struggling in their role every step of the way.

(**Important caution: Before you consider changing *anything* about your hiring practices, be sure to see the important disclaimer on page 41–42 about Equal Employment considerations.**)

**Don't send in the clones:** Avoid hiring a homogenous group of employees; aim for diversity in nearly every aspect of the people you hire, *except* in whether or not they possess the underlying traits that are conducive to great service. Hiring based on traits should help you discover what lies *within* an applicant, allowing you to transcend the biases we all have when "going with our gut," and thereby uncover unexpected future superstars.

**Cast a wide net:** It's hard to hire great employees if you're forced to make your selection from too small a pool of applicants. The solution is ABS (Always Be Scouting): use technology to recruit prospective employees 24/7. If you're doing your screening 24/7, and getting back to prospects in a timely manner, you'll soon find yourself able to select employees from a large and varied pool.

**Unlock the discretionary (optional) efforts of your employees:** Great customer service is contingent on unlocking the optional, *discretionary* efforts of employees—the stuff that's not spelled out in their job description, that they can choose to withhold from, or contribute to, your organization. A good start here is to make sure your employees *know* what you want from them: your aspirations for your organization and for an employee working within it, from orientation (see next paragraph) onward.

**The importance of purpose-focused orientation (onboarding):** Employees are unusually impressionable during their first days on the job. So tell them about your vision; about the purpose of the organization; about what truly matters in providing superior customer service.

**Nurturing employees and monitoring their development:** Make a commitment to systematically develop employees throughout their tenure. Schedule management discussions with each employee at regular intervals to ensure they're progressing in relation to their potential and in relation to their desires for career growth.

**Employees deserve to have input into how their duties are designed and carried out:** Even though you do want to let your employees know *what* needs to get done, you also, when possible, should avoid dictating *how* they need to go about designing their day and carrying out their duties.

**Millennials as employees:** There are infinite individual variations *within* every generation, and it's essential to avoid typecasting any generation as *always* thinking and behaving in a particular way. This applies to all generations, including the millennial generation (born approximately 1980–1996) that is making up more and more of today's workforce. However, millennials do, as a very general rule, tend to share some beliefs and expectations that make them *on average* distinguishable from previous generations. Here are some suggestions for how to respond to these beliefs and expectations:

1. Millennials are hungry for feedback, so give it to them.
2. Millennials want to share responsibility, so find ways to give them some—sooner rather than later.
3. Support millennials' desire for work-life balance.
4. Let millennials work for an ethical organization—by being one.

1. Do the selection (hiring) criteria in our organization give enough weight to personality traits that align with what's needed for customer-facing work, as opposed to previous experience and existing skills? If not, should we move in this direction?

2. Could we be casting a wider net than we do now by offering a round-the-clock online preliminary application portal in order to afford us a larger pool of potential prospects? Would this be a benefit to our organization if implemented?

3. Employee onboarding (orientation): Is ours focused on conveying our organizational purpose and a new employee's part in it, or is it primarily mundane and legalistic? If the latter, what can be done to address this?

4. Do employees have significant input into how their duties are designed and carried out? If not, can this be achieved in our organization? Would it be of value to employee development and morale if it were?

5. Millennials as employees: Micah recommends a set of four accommodations . . .
   - They're hungry for feedback, so give it to them.
   - They want to share responsibility—so find ways to let them.
   - Support their desire for work-life balance.

▪ Let them work for an ethical organization—by being one.

. . . that can make employment more attractive for this large generation of employees. Do you agree with his list? Are there any approaches on this list that we should adopt that we haven't already?

6. Micah also warns against overly generalizing about how the members of any generation think or behave. Do you agree that this is a hazard? Is it a problem in our organization?

Reminder: All of the reading group guides are available as a single document you can download for free at **guides.micahsolomon.com**.

# DIVERSITY AND INCLUSION NOTES FOR CHAPTER 3

FROM MICHAEL HYTER, MANAGING PARTNER
AT KORN FERRY AND AUTHOR OF
*THE POWER OF INCLUSION*

In the preceding chapter on talent management, Micah talks about the danger of "going with your gut" in employee selection, and he's asked me to expand on this in terms of inclusion and diversity.

Going with your gut is an easy way to miss future essential contributors to your organization because you just "know" someone is or isn't going to be a great fit for the position you have in mind. This can be for run-of-the-mill reasons: for example, that you expected someone gregarious and the person you interviewed seems reserved. Although certainly some positions—sales and so forth—benefit from hiring flamboyantly outgoing people, the challenge is that how someone behaves in an interview may not fully represent how they'll interact with customers in a more realistic situation.

But the problem goes well beyond the question of how people interview. We all have mental slots for what we think a person in a particular position will be like. And the more important the position in the organization, the more likely the slot you're reserving mentally is going to be for someone *who's a whole lot like you*. I counsel major corporations on whom to hire for executive positions, and when I suggest they consider someone who doesn't fit what they have in their mental slot, it's very difficult to get them to broaden their thinking.

Failing to be more inclusive in your thinking leads to reduced opportunities for people who are browner/more female/more disabled/younger/older/more foreign-seeming/more southern/more northern, and so forth in an organization. But I'm not trying to sell you this inclusive thinking only for altruistic reasons. It's also a huge loss for your organization if you don't consider someone for the C-suite who has all the other qualifications but is, say, thirty-three when you expected someone in their fifties. Or, in tech, someone in their fifties when you expected a thirty-three-year-old. Or someone to sell pharmaceuticals who doesn't look like the perfectly toothed, pencil-thin model types you're used to hiring. Or someone for your front desk who uses a wheelchair. Because with this kind of restricted thinking, you greatly restrict your talent pool; you're no longer picking the best of the best; you're picking the best, potentially, of the mediocre. And this is a loss for you, your customers, and your bottom line.

# THE POWER OF "WOW": CREATING STORIES THAT CUSTOMERS WILL REMEMBER—AND SPREAD

One message I don't enjoy delivering to my clients (although some of them seem convinced that it gives me some kind of sick pleasure) is my tough-love mantra that *satisfactory customer service isn't enough.* Although it's essential to consistently offer competent, reliable customer service—and to invest in the standards, systems, and training that it takes to pull this off—don't sell your company short by stopping there. If you want to create the kind of passionate customer engagement that will turn your company into a legend of service and win you customers for life, you need to take your efforts one step beyond. You need to pursue what I call "wow."

A wow experience is *when service goes beyond fulfilling basic customer expectations and does so in a creative, unexpected way.* By creating a wow experience, you give rise to a story in the mind of your customer. Since humans tend to think and remember in terms of stories, the wow approach is one of the most effective ways to build lasting connections with customers. These wow stories have a good likelihood of living on in memory, encouraging customers to not only return, but to share their memories of the experience with friends, family, and coworkers—and, through social media, the world.

Rob Siefker, the senior director of the contact center at Zappos, a company whose stated purpose is "to live and deliver WOW," offers the example of a Zappos employee who took the initiative required to create a wow moment—and build an indelible customer memory:

> Not long ago, two of our customers—a newly married couple—were packing up their belongings to move to a new home, and, in the rush of the move, the husband packed his wife's jewelry inside one of her purses and then packed the purse inside what he thought was a spare Zappos box. His wife, it turns out, was intending to return that purse to Zappos using that very box, which she then did, having no idea that inside the purse now were several thousand dollars' worth of her jewelry!
>
> When the couple arrived at their new home and started to unpack, bedlam broke out as the wife figured out what had happened—and as it sunk in that her jewelry was, perhaps irretrievably, missing. The rep she reached out to at Zappos decided to reroute the box directly to his own desk and then, fearing for the safety of the valuables in transit were he to ship them, purchased a plane ticket [yes, Zappos repaid him] so he could hand-deliver the package himself.
>
> When he and the jewelry arrived, the grateful couple invited him in for dinner. They're now customers for life, as you can imagine.

## "Wow" Isn't Always a Grand Production: How Zappos Creates "Everyday Wow" on Every Call

The story of the purse and jewelry is a particularly dramatic example. Not all moments of wow need to be so over the top. *A wow connection can also be achieved less theatrically through the use of the right words in conversation with a customer, words that make an emotional connection that transcends the transactional.* Although this is a less dramatic form of wow, it can be similarly powerful.

Even at Zappos, for every Hollywood-ending story like the jewelry rescue, there are hundreds more instances where what I call "everyday wow" is delivered, typically over the phone, the humble vessel that Zappos considers to be its most important connection with customers. In fact, Zappos commits itself to delivering wow, or at least a wow attempt, on *every* phone call fielded by an employee in its contact center.

"We want to distinguish the service experience for every customer, on each and every phone call," says Megan Petrini, a customer service training facilitator for Zappos. "The connection can be anything, as long as it authentically relates to the customer. If you hear a dog bark [in the background on the customer's end of a call], you can connect over your shared love of animals. If you hear a kid in the background, ditto." Or (and this is perhaps most common), you can connect over the details of the customer's order or the particular question or difficulty that has them calling in—by taking the conversation somewhere beyond a "just the facts" approach.

## Eavesdropping on Zappos

Let's listen in on Madison, an experienced and proficient Zappos employee who's working the phones. A customer calls in who is at her wit's end over the challenges of finding a comfortable shoe in a narrow size for an upcoming family wedding. Madison responds with great empathy and passion:

> Honestly, "narrows" are the worst! It's almost like the whole industry has conspired against people with narrow feet. My aunt has narrow feet like you, and I swear it seems like every other conversation I have with her is about her miseries related to them.

As you can imagine, the two of them are soon besties. And, quickly, Madison's customer regains hope that the upcoming wedding will be something other than a torture-fest for her feet. Then, browsing together while still on the call, Madison and the customer manage to find a new, likely candidate for pain-free but dressy footwear.

On calls with other customers, Madison will, depending on the customer and context, deliver wow by upgrading shipping so that shoes will arrive in time for a special event, or by gifting a customer with a duplicate order of shoes they've received, so they can donate them to a favored charity or give them to a friend, rather than going through the hassle of returning them. And, she can occasionally be caught sending flowers to a customer who is bereaved—or, who is celebrating a happy occasion.

## The Importance of Breathing Space When You're Striving to Create "Wow"

What Madison does for her customers—taking all the time needed to bond with them on the phone; maybe sending them a small gift or comping them one of the items in their order—may or may not cost Zappos any money; certainly, it doesn't cost them a lot. And, as a general rule, "everyday wow" customer service doesn't have to cost money, at least not directly. But what it does require is *breathing space*.

You can find the kind of breathing space that's conducive to creating wow moments reflected in the metrics of the Zappos contact center. Zappos runs at just 60 to 70 percent agent occupancy rather than following the industry norm, which is somewhere in the 80s, according to the latest figures from contact center specialist Colin Taylor of Taylor Reach. (Agent occupancy is the percentage of time that call center agents spend—or are predicted to spend—handling calls, as a percentage of the time they are on the clock.)

Why is this contact center overstaffing so important? When your bottom line is, as it is at Zappos, to make an emotional connection with each caller, the resulting conversations create great *variability* in call length. An emotional connection can take just a moment: maybe a quick second of bonding "over both being named Megan without an *h*—which is the sensible spelling, of course!" which is an example that Megan (no *h*), the workshop facilitator, is fond of sharing from her personal experience. Or, it could be an *extended* discussion of a tragedy recently experienced by the customer. (This situation crops up more often than you'd expect, particularly when a Zappos employee ends up on the line with a grieving widow or widower who's not sure what to do with recently ordered shoes intended for a spouse or partner who has died since the order was placed.)

Breathing space is an essential element in what happens *leading up to* that wow moment as well, the moment when the agent makes the connection with a live customer on the line: When you're hiring for wow, you need the breathing space (time) to find people with an aptitude for making emotional connections with customers, and training for wow requires ample time before you can put employees face to face (or voice to voice) with customers.

## How The Ritz-Carlton Hotel Company Creates "Wow"

A few hundred miles from Zappos, wow is also on the agenda at Dove Mountain, a Ritz-Carlton resort in the Arizona desert, where a family of three is wrapping up its weekend getaway. Asked to come down to the lobby "for a minute," the guests find themselves escorted out the door and into the desert twilight by a group of smiling employees for what reveals itself to be an elaborate, *Hobbit*-themed quest, clandestinely put together for them by these very same employees. The staff, it turns out, made note of two specific details about the family back when they checked in: that their kid is celebrating a birthday, and is passionate about everything having to do with J. R. R. Tolkien. Working with just those two pieces of data, "the hotel employees used them to completely transform our stay," says the mom of the family, "to make us feel like the most special people in the world."

The scenario was as follows: Setting out on a path that runs through the sprawling property, the questing party would happen upon ancient-looking scrolls along the way that had been done up with hand-drawn calligraphy, each scroll providing another clue or instruction. The quest culminated in a dramatic moment where they witnessed wooden barrels, filled with what looked like dwarves, fly down a waterfall (just a water slide at the resort's pool, but in the deepening twilight, the illusion worked) and were invited to shoot arrows at a "dragon" (actually a piñata) from which a large pile of gold (foil-wrapped chocolate coins) poured out on impact, all of which mimicked famous scenes from *The Hobbit* and left the guests awestruck.

*There's solid business logic behind such elaborate, creative efforts*, which is good, because the efforts required *can* be extensive: In the case of the *Hobbit*-themed adventure, it required the employees who created it to take time away from their general duties, read up on Tolkien, recruit other employees to help stage the adventure on the property, and conspire to gather the family together at just the right time—twilight—to enjoy the magic. "Our goal is to create indelible marks through the work we do at the property level," explains Lisa Holladay, vice president and global brand leader for the Ritz-Carlton Hotel Company, as well as other marquee brands in the Marriott luxury lineup, "that will live on for our guests and become family lore or legend." Over and over, "we see the power this has in bringing guests closer to our brand in a way that lasts for years, even for a lifetime."

This culture of striving for wow benefits employee morale and retention as well, through what you might call a spillover effect. Says Holladay, "We also have wow stories that happen internally. We're not famous [among the general public] for these," unlike the customer-facing wow stories, "because they're internal, but I hear many times that 'these are the reasons I stay with the Ritz-Carlton as an employee.'" For example, she's heard many comments such as this one: "When my wife was coming through surgery, my friends who work here stocked my fridge and helped me with the driving; my work colleagues are some of the most hospitable people in my personal life as well."

## IS "WOW" EXPENSIVE? ONLY IF YOU'RE LOUSY AT MATH.

Any time someone tells you that wow customer service is too expensive, *ask them how much they paid on their marketing and sales efforts last year.* Creating an emotional connection with your customers is the most direct route to getting your customers to *do your marketing for you.* And I'm talking about powerful, credible marketing that, unlike many traditional marketing approaches, tends to grow and grow, rather than to fade out without additional infusions of cash.

In spite of this, one of the main reasons that a wow approach fails to take root or be sustained at most companies is that success here requires the support of an entire organization, all the way up to the highest levels of leadership. Consider how attractive it will look to a shortsighted leader or

manager to *under*staff a contact center, or to loosen up on hiring require-
ments, or to shorten the training period before newly hired employees
encounter a live customer.

To a penny pinching manager or shareholder, the elements required
to create wow look expensive. *But c'mon!* The reality is that winning and
retaining customers this way is one of the only true bargains around,
because of the word of mouth it inspires.

It's hard to find good data on the percentage of customers who rely on
word of mouth, especially digital word of mouth. The most credible recent
numbers go as high as 93 percent* for percentage of customers who rely,
at least to some extent, on word of mouth.

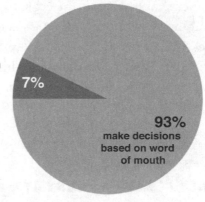

**93%** of
customers say
they make
decisions based in
full or in part on
word-of-mouth
recommendations

7%

93%
make decisions
based on word
of mouth

Figure 4.1

That 93 percent figure sounds about right to me. But quickly I started
wondering who the holdouts could possibly be, the stubborn 7 percent who
*never* listen to word of mouth.

Then I figured it out—it's just one guy; it's my uncle! He might occasionally check *Consumer Reports*, but that's it; other than that he listens
to no one.

---

* There is some nuance to coming up with such a number, which I've distilled from several
sources; I admit it's art and opinion more than it's pure science.

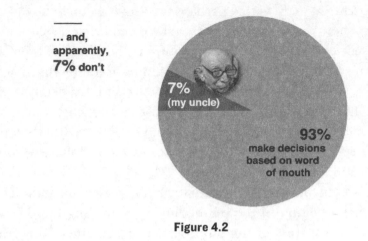

... and,
apparently,
7% don't

7%
(my uncle)

93%
make decisions
based on word
of mouth

Figure 4.2

## When "Wow" Is Achieved via Simple Human Thoughtfulness

It's a mistake to think that wow customer service is always a dramatic "reveal" like the *Hobbit*-themed birthday surprise. Wow can also be achieved *even if the customer can see the magic as it's being created*. This next case is an example of this. It again takes place at a Ritz-Carlton property, but this time, the main ingredient required to pull off wow is simple human thoughtfulness.

A friend of mine is the father of a nine-year-old boy with multiple, potentially life-threatening, food allergies. These are the kind of allergies that require my friend and his wife to bring an EpiPen—and a lot of parental anxiety—along with them wherever the family travels.

The family decided to set off for Hong Kong recently, a destination much farther from the family's native San Francisco than the family had ventured previously. *(I've changed a few identifying details to protect the son's privacy.)*

The wrinkle was this: How, in a land of exotic cuisines, would they manage to keep their son safe, while also allowing themselves a bit of relaxation as a couple; a chance to let their guards down?

It occurred to them that perhaps the Ritz-Carlton hotel in Hong Kong, where they were planning to stay, would have a solution. So, they sent a letter to the property, outlining the details of their son's multiple allergies and asking if he could be accommodated.

They were *floored* by the response they received: a detailed letter from the office of Peter Find, the hotel's executive chef, with a comprehensive listing of the foods that could be prepared to meet their son's needs, dishes that ranged from exotic local Chinese recipes to familiar foods like pasta.

"It was encouraging and actually kind of amazing—the chef's personal attention in responding and in providing that list, and the thoughtfulness of the food options it contained," my friend tells me. "This was *good* stuff—stuff that our son would actually be likely to enjoy. And, in fact, at mealtimes in the hotel, enjoyment is exactly what I saw: our son enjoying himself, not being stuck eating something austere, but really digging in and being a kid, a happy kid, enthusiastically chowing down."

## Thermos-Enabled Day Trips

The culinary staff's thoughtfulness improved the family's enjoyment beyond the confines of the hotel as well. "The kitchen staff prepared a Thermos for us each day, full of hot food that our son could eat, which allowed us to take day trips all over Hong Kong. That may not sound like much, but it transformed our visit, taking a huge worry off of our shoulders as parents and freeing us up to have adventures as a family in this city that was foreign to us."

## It's Not about the Glitz and Glamour

I hope my friend's story will help clarify what wow customer service is all about—and what it's not. Although the story took place in a luxury hotel, I want to point out that *nothing in the story depended on glitz and glamour.* And, in talking with the family about their experience in Hong Kong, I didn't hear a peep about sparkling swimming pools, blown-glass chandeliers, or the billion-dollar views commanded by the hotel. What mattered is that their kid was able to be a kid, they were able to relax as parents, and they all felt cared for. Now *that* is a wow.

## Anticipatory Customer Service: A Powerful (and Magical) Force

The other point I hope to convey with this example is the power of what I call "anticipatory customer service," which means answering a question or fulfilling a need that a customer *hasn't even voiced,* perhaps because the customer "doesn't want to be a bother" or doesn't know enough about the subject to formulate a request in words, or doesn't even realize that they have such a need.

Anticipatory customer service is what the culinary staff was providing in Hong Kong when they packed the daily Thermos *without* being asked to do so, *without* the guest family even quite figuring out that this was a need they had or that this was a service that, realistically, the hotel could be asked to provide. *Striving to be anticipatory elevates your service level in a way that is memorable and meaningful. And it's very likely to be a direct path to wowing your customers.*

## Selecting "Wow-Capable" Employees

At Zappos, when employees are hired to work with customers, it's not the employees' existing skill set or previous work experience that matter as much as their natural affinity for people and service. The same holds true for the culinary staff that served the boy with allergies at the Hong Kong Ritz-Carlton and for the junior employees who created the *Hobbit* quest at the Dove Mountain resort. By hiring employees who are equipped temperamentally for delighting customers (as discussed in the previous chapter), an organization takes an essential step toward the creation of wow. Recruiting and selecting such employees, the ones who have an affinity for making connections with—and making a difference for—every customer they encounter, provides the raw material necessary to give wow a chance of happening.

## IT'S NOT ALWAYS THE RIGHT TIME FOR "WOW"

Once you task your employees with creating wow, you should *ready yourself for some awkward and not quite appropriate applications* of the principle until they understand the nuances required for success.

For starters, it can be hard for newly energized employees to understand that *customers don't always have time to be wowed.* Customers are often in a rush, and it's important that employees learn to tone down or cut short their efforts to turn every basic interaction into a wow experience, if they're getting signals from a customer that they're under time constraints. It's also important that employee efforts at wow don't run afoul of a customer's desire to stay within their own private bubble, a bubble that an employee *shouldn't even attempt to enter* if a customer is glued to a personal communication device, interacting intently with their family or colleagues, trying to get work done, or otherwise occupied or preoccupied in such a way that an extended interaction would be seen as intrusive.

## Recognizing and Rewarding Employees' Efforts toward "Wow"

It's important to reward the efforts that employees make toward creating wow, yet I hesitate to bring up the subject of rewards for fear of being misunderstood. I'm *not* primarily talking about a scheme of financial rewards and prizes. While small, targeted prizes can be fun, a complex system for financially rewarding wow is likely to quickly become nothing better than a distraction. Plus, employees are smart people (often smarter than their bosses), and reward systems along those lines are often gamed faster than the boss can blink.

What I mean by "rewarding wow" is more as follows: *take a look at how you react when employees go the extra mile for your customers.* You can either express your disapproval by punishing employees for what they did, on the grounds that the extra assistance they provided to a customer took extra time and reduced the employee's (narrowly defined) productivity, or you can *celebrate* their actions and recognize them as heroes. The choice is yours, and it can make all the difference.

For a good model, look at how employees at the Ritz-Carlton Hotel Company are recognized for their efforts and creativity after they create a memorable experience for their guests. Twice a week (Monday and Friday), at every Ritz-Carlton hotel and resort, the company shares a wow story from one of its more than one hundred properties, something striking that an employee at one of these hotels recently did for a guest. The intention is to inspire other employees to find ways to do something similarly memorable for their own guests, to say to themselves, "You know what? That wasn't that difficult. I could do that too," says Holladay, the Ritz-Carlton vice president.

And look at what *doesn't* happen: In the *Hobbit* example, the Ritz-Carlton Dove Mountain employees *aren't* criticized for going off-property to buy items needed to create the *Hobbit* quest; in the case of the boy with the serious allergies, the Hong Kong culinary team *isn't* chided for paying too much attention to the needs of one single boy, such as taking time out of their morning routine to prepare a travel Thermos for him when that same time could certainly be applied to working on the morning rush of room service orders.

## Empower Your Employees If You Want Them to Create "Wow"

Any efforts you make to encourage the creation of wow will quickly run aground unless you empower employees to take the initiative (creative and sometimes financial) that can be required. The employee at Zappos who traveled personally to return the customer's lost jewelry, the employees at Dove Mountain who developed the *Hobbit*-themed quest, and the chefs in Hong Kong who created the allergen-free menu were all acting out scenarios that would have been impossible without empowerment.

Employees can only pull off extraordinary acts on behalf of a customer if they have a meaningful level of on-the-job empowerment: *the power to make decisions in favor of a customer*. Most of this manifests itself in nonfinancial ways such as the choices that employees make for how to invest their time on the job. However, an element of fiscal autonomy is important as well if employees are going to be able to deliver wow on the spot, without hesitation and without having to ask for the approval of a manager. At Zappos, this financial leeway is relatively modest, yet sufficient to allow, for example, comping a modestly priced pair of shoes or providing coupons for free or discounted items. At the Ritz-Carlton Hotel Company, the financial empowerment of *every employee* is much greater. The company both allows and even *encourages* its employees, once they're fully trained, to use up to a theoretical $2,000 per guest to solve a problem or to improve a guest's stay.

## A TRICKY THING ABOUT EMPOWERMENT

When every single employee is empowered to solve absolutely any customer issue, you'd think all customers would be similarly delighted, no matter which employee they happen to be talking with. The problem is that, for decades, crummy, overly hierarchical businesses have

> taught consumers that the only way to get satisfaction is to demand to be transferred to a supervisor. When a customer makes this demand at your (non-crummy) business, how should your frontline employee react? Saying over and over, "There's no need to be transferred to a supervisor; I have the same tools and leeway my supervisor would have to assist you, Ms. Smith," doesn't really work if Ms. Smith continues to demand, more and more emphatically, to talk to a supervisor. Better is to do what Zappos does: create a "resource desk" that customers who refuse to let an empowered frontline employee solve their problems can be transferred to. The employees at the resource desk don't have any additional leeway beyond what the frontline Zappos employees have, but they can offer a new voice and a new set of ears, which is sometimes all that a customer needs to hear and be heard by.

Before you throw my book against the wall or into the shredder, let me repeat: This $2,000 figure is truly just theoretical. *No Ritz-Carlton employee has ever needed to make use of the entire amount of their discretionary spending ability.* But *the openness and relaxed attitude* that come about when any Ritz-Carlton employee—a housekeeper, a landscaper—knows that the company's leaders trust them so completely that they could, if need be, spend $2,000 on a customer's behalf, without retaliation (or even raised eyebrows), is a massive boost to employee engagement and sparks great creativity among the employees in the organization on behalf of their customers.

Herve Humler, the Ritz-Carlton Hotel Company's cofounder, put it to me this way: Ritz-Carlton employees "have total power, and all the resources of our organization, to create these moments, these stories, on their own, without needing to ask permission, without needing to involve management, without needing to worry that they're going too far. The time spent creating these stories isn't time *taken out of* their job; this time spent *is* their job."

Can you picture the words you've just read being spoken, sincerely, within your own organization? Do the top leaders at *your* company encourage employees to get busy finding opportunities to do *more* work, on the clock, for your customers, and perhaps spend *more* of the company's money to take care of them? I doubt it, which is too bad, because, if they would only try it, they'd be sending a very powerful message.

Now, if discretionary spending of up to $2,000 a day per employee per customer sounds impossible—ridiculous, even—in the context of your own business, I encourage you to find a different limit that works within your own business context. *The amount of money involved isn't the point.* What matters is that employees be broadly empowered to assist customers and to do so immediately, without the need to ask for approval from those higher up in their organization.

Such is the case at CHROME, a federal credit union in Washington, Pennsylvania, that's frequently ranked high in its market for member satisfaction ("member" being the term for customers in the credit-union world). Not long ago, two CHROME employees, Jon and Sarah, headed out to a member's home to help him get signed up, in person, for a new online banking service. (They had tried previously to work through the online setup with this particular member on the phone, without success. But having him come in to the branch to get signed up wasn't going to work either, as the mountainous area where CHROME is located was suffering through a period of extreme weather and weather-related road hazards.)

When they arrived at the member's home, he confided that he'd been having "a rough time" with the recent rainstorms and flooding, both because they were limiting his ability to get around and because his basement was prone to flooding. "We peeked in the basement door," says Jon from CHROME, "and saw what I'd say was a *foot* of water that he'd been trying to bail out using buckets. He did know there was a better way and, in fact, showed me an ad for a Shop-Vac pump that he was going to buy once his next Social Security payment went into his account, which wouldn't happen for another two weeks."

Jon and Sarah decided on the spot that they were going to buy him the Shop-Vac and then drove to the local supply store to get what turned out to be the last one still in stock, which they were able to buy using the CHROME company credit card that is available for such occasions. According to Robert Flanyak, the president and CEO of CHROME, "This solution did require a financial outlay, and when a solution does require one, the use of the company credit card is intended, even encouraged, as a resource. There's no set limit; we just request that our employees use sound judgment."

"I want to take pains to mention, though, that there are cases I'm equally proud of where our employees made an exceptional effort for our 17,000 members by investing something other than money: a bit of creativity and expertise, applied where it could make a difference. For example, we've had employees roll up their sleeves and work side by side with a member on family budgeting after their income had dropped precipitously. *Something like that doesn't depend on cash at all, but it can make all the difference to a member.*"

## "WEDDING RING OVERBOARD!": "WOW" CUSTOMER SERVICE, A HUNDRED MILES FROM SHORE

Seabourn Cruise Line, a Seattle-based operator of luxury cruises, finds ways to pursue wow hundreds of miles from solid ground: out on the high seas, where resources tend to be more limited and the challenges more pronounced than they are ashore.

Richard D. (Rick) Meadows, the president of Seabourn, tells me:

Our mission at Seabourn pivots on one key word, and that is the word "moments." "Moments," at Seabourn, are those connection points where we interact with a guest [passenger]. These are our opportunities to excel, and to provide something that's beyond what our guests would expect. This approach is at the core for us; it's something we're wired to do across the board on all ships. And it's also something that we're conscious of doing across our crews. In other words, exceptional moments happen among crew members as well, when they interact with each other.

What I call "wow moments" (and Meadows simply calls "moments") can be small and subtle, or they can be large and dramatic. There was the time when a passenger's shoe came apart and a crew member polled her colleagues until she found a pair that was the right size for the guest to borrow. And there's the passenger who was on her way to a celebration dinner when her dress had a malfunction all the way up and down the back. "Very quickly," says Meadows, the suite stewardess rallied the tailor. "They sewed her into her dress as quickly and delicately as they could, so she could go down to dinner and not miss the event."

Meadows then hit me with one final example of a moment in the Seabourn customer experience that was neither small nor subtle.

"We had a guest who was heading out for a shore excursion with her husband, putting on hand lotion as she left her suite. As she walked out to the gangway, she was rubbing the lotion in when her wedding ring flew off—beyond the gangway and into the water."

Micah: "That sounds pretty final."

Rick: "It *looked* pretty final. These are deep waters. Our guest was very upset, distraught even. As it happened, the captain was on the gangway for another reason. So he told our guest, 'Look, go on your shore excursion. When you come back I'll make sure that we do all the claims reporting with you to make this [insurance replacement] process as easy as possible.'

The minute the guest was out of sight, however, the captain sprang into action with another plan entirely. He took it upon himself to contact some divers in the waters nearby, to ask them to find the ring. Which, against all odds, they were able to do.

Once the ringless guest was back on board, a crewmember telephoned her suite and asked her to come to the ship's common area, 'to fill out the insurance paperwork.' But as she arrived, the captain came up to her and said, 'I think I have something for you—is this what you're looking for?' and held up the ring."

# READER'S CHEATSHEET
# FOR CHAPTER 4

*A wow experience is when a service provided to a customer goes beyond ful-filling basic expectations and does so in a creative, unexpected way.* Wow can be a powerful way to connect emotionally with a customer. The wow stories created by the experience are likely to live on in the customer's memory as well as being shared enthusiastically with the customer's friends and contacts.

Furthermore, the act of creating wow, and the feeling of being empowered by the organization to do so, can inspire the employees involved and be a powerful tool for improving teamwork, employee retention, and companywide morale.

If you want to wow your customers, here's how to do it:

1. Empower your employees to make on-the-spot wow decisions *without* having to run to a manager for

approval, even if these decisions require financial out-
lays or investments of time.

2. Actively recruit and hire wow-capable employees, as
discussed in more detail in chapter 3.

3. When your employees make an effort to wow customers,
publicly recognize and applaud their contributions.

4. Encourage your employees to practice *anticipatory
customer service*, which means answering a question or
fulfilling a need or desire that a customer hasn't even
voiced—because they're shy, because they don't want
to betray their ignorance, because they don't know the
extent of how you can help them, or simply because
they don't understand enough to put their request into
words. Anticipatory customer service is one of the most
effective ways to create wow.

5. Be sensitive to when it's the right and wrong time to
wow your customers; a customer who is in a rush or
is busy with a business call or a personal conversation
isn't going to appreciate the disruption, no matter how
well intended.

6. Keep in mind that not all wow moments are the result
of elaborate actions. They can also be created through
the use of the right words in conversation with a customer, words that make an emotional connection that
transcends the transactional. For example, Zappos
employees strive to make a connection on every single
phone call by bonding over something relatively work-
aday (a love of pets) or dramatic (a more serious shared
interest/concern) based on cues the employee picks up
on from the customer.

1. Do we have a stated or implied goal at our organization of providing wow to customers (even if we don't use the "wow" word), of delivering service that goes beyond the expected and transactional, and is designed to make an emotional connection with our customers?

2. If not, would such a goal be of value to our organization? And does it seem realistic for us to pursue it?

3. Assuming the answers to #1 and #2 are, respectively, "no" (not currently committed to wow) and "yes" (we do want to commit), what are some steps we could take to explicitly commit to wow and to begin our journey to get there? For example: modify our mission statement; change or supplement employee training to promote and train for wow; add reinforcement rituals to celebrate employees who succeed in creating wow.

4. Do you agree with Micah that it's credible to believe that 93 percent of customers listen to word of mouth (or digital "word of thumb") when making a purchasing decision? (Extra credit: do you remember which of Micah's relatives represents the other 7 percent?)

Reminder: All of the reading group guides are available as a single document you can download for free at **guides.micahsolomon.com**.

**5**

# THE EXPERIENCE MEANS EVERYTHING

I t's hard to streamline your way into a customer's heart. Even though streamlining (reducing friction, minimizing clicks or steps, improving efficiency) is undeniably important in pleasing today's customers, it's just as true that many customers, much of the time, are hoping for more than well-oiled minimalism. They're looking for the customer experience to *be* an experience.

*Think of the ideal customer experience as a movie you're putting on for your customers, a movie that requires your attention to cinematic details such as continuity, casting, lighting, and soundtrack.* If you get these right, your customers will likely find themselves caught up in the storyline and swept away by the feelings that have been created.

## Customer Experience as Cinema: Doin' It Like Drybar

A cinematic approach is central to the success of Drybar, the blow-drying and hairstyling phenomenon that has transformed the hair care landscape across North America, growing over the course of a decade from a basement operation to 125 locations in the United States and Canada. Drybar's success is particularly impressive because it shows that the company manages to engage their customers and succeed as a company with what might look, at first glance, like nothing much to write home about.

To the uninitiated, it's easy to scoff that Drybar has no business charging $45 for simply washing your hair and blowing it dry. But judging from Drybar's runaway success, it's clear that the company is offering more than meets the eye. Clients (nearly 3,000,000 times a year!) visit Drybar locations and return week after week not only for the haircare results, but because their time spent at Drybar offers an immersive experience, an elaborate movie that Drybar has put on for their benefit. This experience—this movie—is what has allowed Drybar to expand rapidly, build an extremely loyal clientele, and keep knockoffs at bay–despite a business model that looks, superficially, like an easy target (a sitting duck, really) for any upstart competitor with a hairdryer, a sink, and some forearm strength.

*"The experience is everything,"* says Drybar cofounder Michael Landau, who started the business alongside his sister, Alli Webb (it was Alli's basement in which they started). "If it weren't for the experience we create, we would just be another place styling women's hair. What we're selling at Drybar is a feeling and an experience: for forty-five minutes, you get to relax and be pampered, drinking a mimosa and indulging in the guilty pleasure of the latest chick flick or celebrity magazine while someone washes and brushes your hair."

Drybar's craft reveals itself in dozens of little details as the "movie" progresses. There's the swift, seamless online booking process and the expert, congenial pre-blowout consultation. Telephone hold times are tracked and kept to a minimum. The menu of blowout styles is engagingly written, with each option named after a different cocktail. The Mai Tai blowout is described as "effortless, messy, beachy hair," while the Southern Comfort promises "big hair and lots of volume."

The décor at Drybar is stylish; the furnishings are comfortable and extraordinarily well thought out. (Each salon chair has its own purse hook!) All the films that Drybar screens on the monitors found throughout their spaces (romantic comedies, of course) have been carefully vetted and are captioned with subtitles so the volume can be kept moderate and prevent customers from suffering from auditory overload. The salon's music playlist is so distinctive that Drybar has even been able to market it as a commercial album release. (In contrast to many businesses, which overlook the importance of sound, getting this right is an obsession at Drybar. Most fundamentally, they've figured out how to attenuate the sound that their custom-designed blow-dryers make, to keep them from roaring like lawnmowers and drowning out the rest of the activity "on set.")

And, in a particularly theatrical touch where Drybar diverges from standard salon procedure, clients are seated so they face *away* from the mirror until the very last minute, when they're spun around for a signature "reveal" at the end. This serves for dramatic effect and to improve the blowout experience for both the client and the stylist. Cofounder Alli Webb discovered, back when Drybar was still in her basement, that clients relax more and micromanage the process less when they're not looking at their damp, not-yet-perfectly coiffed hair mid-blowout.

### Perplexing but True: Customers Can Love an Experience— Without Being Able to Tell You Why

Although I've been laying out the elements of the cinematic customer experience, with Drybar as an example, one by one, don't get me wrong: The many small elements of a great customer experience are unlikely to be recalled later on in individual detail by the customers who've enjoyed them. Even though I've broken out these individual components so that you can see how the whole experience has been created, if you were to ask the average Drybar customer what they loved about their visit, the answer will likely be closer to "it was great" than to a more specific and useful answer like, "The hair dryers were quiet, and I didn't have to worry about how my hairstyle was progressing until the very end, because I couldn't see the mirror until then."

## THE *EMPLOYEE* EXPERIENCE POWERS THE CUSTOMER EXPERIENCE—AND YOU CAN'T EVER TAKE IT FOR GRANTED

The last thing you might expect to find inside a hypergrowth tech company is an utterly serene, supportive internal atmosphere. Yet that's the experience on offer for employees and visitors alike within the headquarters of Nextiva, the business communications company that I introduced previously. And this is more than a surface-level phenomenon, says Yaniv Masjedi, Nextiva's CMO.

Masjedi, a member of the team who founded Nextiva more than a decade ago, says that "all of the key players who were in the office when we got our first customer, on May 15, 2008, are still working here," continuing to drive a company that remains true to its core even in the face of a growth rate that, some years, reaches as high as 500 percent.

The secret to both the pace of growth and the feet-on-the ground atmosphere at Nextiva "comes down to a culture where all of us are on the same page when it comes to focusing on providing our signature Amazing Service, externally as well as internally."

Nextiva's customer-oriented culture flows directly from the company's origin story. The brand was built in response to a customer service letdown that the founders suffered in their previous entrepreneurial careers. "Tomas [Gorny, Nextiva's CEO] had the idea for Nextiva in response to challenges that we'd had ourselves at a precursor company in our own attempts to acquire a sensible, effective phone system for our own business," says

Masjedi. "It was a sorry scene: After doing a ton of research, we'd had to plop down over a quarter million dollars to buy a phone system for our office—and here was the kicker: As soon as we deployed it, we were even more miserable than before. It was difficult to manage, difficult to use, expensive—there were fees on top of fees on top of fees—and overall it was simply a drag. But it was also an opportunity: If *we* were having this problem, we knew *other* businesses were running into the same issues. We started conceptualizing what became Nextiva, a company with a mission of simplifying business communication and that always kept the customer at the center," a business model that has led Nextiva to handle every customer support call in-house, even today when the company supports over 150,000 clients, including many marquee brands and household names.

As far as a culture of *internal* customer service—the devotion to others within the Nextiva headquarters and in its rapidly growing stable of satellite offices in the US and overseas—this cultural commitment is evident as well. For example, there's the weekly video-based "newsletter," dubbed NexTV.

The NexTV video program isn't the kind of well-intentioned but deadly dull undertaking you may have seen at other companies; a big yawn that employees look forward to not watching every week. Far from it. At Nextiva, they go whole hog producing a new NexTV episode every week (they recently made episode 350!) using professional video equipment and a pair of cheeky interviewers who are devoted to introducing Nextiva employees to each other via interviews that ask truly hard to answer (and endless to ponder) questions, like, "What would you rather be for the rest of your life: itchy or sticky?" which draw engaged responses like, "Before I answer, HOW sticky are we talking?" and, "Would this itch be treatable with a powder?" Masjedi explains the impetus behind NexTV: "It's a unique show. It's filmed by us and can involve absolutely anyone at any of our offices. We use it as a forum to communicate company updates, talk about what is ahead, what's happened, get everyone on the same page. We're well aware that one of the top complaints you hear in many companies is communication: 'I want to know what's going on. They do things without telling me. Oh, this happened, that happened, and I had no clue until after the fact.'

> We really try to get in front of that. NexTV is a key way we've found to effectively communicate throughout the company; it's fun, and we never, ever miss a week."

Even though it's not possible to count on customers to recall or dissect individual elements of a seamlessly constructed whole, the sum of multiple details is what creates the kind of success that Drybar has had—repeatable success, now demonstrated location after location, experience after experience, across North America.

That a customer can have a cinematic experience so immersive and affecting that they can't wait to experience it again—yet not be able to recall, without very specific prompting, what made that experience amazing, is a frustrating reality for anyone in business to consider. Yet, this lack of precise awareness is a reality that shouldn't be glossed over. It's better to recognize this ambiguity than to create false positives—based on wishful thinking—in the face of nebulous data. And this ambiguity is a phenomenon that you'll find yourself coming up against again and again: *How customers perceive and experience your business—how it feels to them and what it means to them—is rarely as simple as those of us who design and deploy customer experiences would like it to be.* For one thing, a customer experience is made up of a dazzling number of impressions: the temperature; the scent; the lighting; the cleanliness of the parking lot; the speed of service; the noise level; the demeanor, tone of voice, and word choice of the employees; and on and on and on. For another, *you're always at the mercy of what the individual customer brings to the equation*—the idiosyncratic ways that a *customer's own* sensibilities and that customer's *own* prior experiences affect their interpretation of what you offer.

These personal connotations that a customer brings to your establishment can be positive or negative. A hospital, although clean, sunlit, and bedecked with plants and artwork, will, for some visitors with tragic prior healthcare experiences, unavoidably evoke death, pain, and mortality. A traditional hardware store, even the most haphazardly managed and maintained, might have the good fortune to evoke a customer's childhood days when their dad, a carpenter, took them to a similar store years ago on errands.

This doesn't mean I'm going to come into your business and tell you to give up on your efforts to improve the sights, sounds, scents, and other details of the customer experience. (I'm actually the guy who'll encourage you to redouble these efforts!) My goal in bringing up these issues is something different: to get you to stop thinking so linearly about the customer experience—to stop pretending that 1 + 1 invariably equals 2 in the mind of the customer. The equations involved are much more complicated and fluid than that. What creates a pleasing result for one customer on one day may be a mismatch for another customer on another day, or even for the same customer later on the same day, perhaps due to something as ephemeral as the dimming light in the late afternoon. And analyzing dimming daylight and its effect on emotions is a realm that requires the best of your poetic impulses alongside the best of your data crunching.

## The Customer Experience Is about Making Your Customer Look Good, Not about Making Your Business Look Good

A great customer experience is one where customers feel their best during the time they spend with you. (There are a few exceptions to this rule, such as physical therapy, personal training "boot camp," and the like, where the overriding goal needs to be how the customer/patient/client will feel *down the road*, and their feelings during the time that they're in your presence should be optimized in ways that don't detract from those ultimate results.) And an important part of "feeling your best" is self-esteem: looking good in your own eyes.

Here are a few questions to gauge how you're making your customers feel.

- *Have you taken a recent, hard look at whether your service or product is easy to use and well-explained (or self-explanatory)?* When a customer struggles with a counterintuitive or poorly explained process or interface, it's not going to make them feel good.

- When a customer is wrong—as we all know, this happens!—*do you bluntly school them in the error of their ways,* or do you make the mistake seem minor and like it could easily have been made by anyone? Or, best of all, do you simply not point the error out to them in the first place, assuming there are no health or safety implications to what they've gotten wrong and the danger that they'll later repeat this error?

- What about actually *getting* to your business? Is it clear where your business is located, where to park, and how to get from the parking spot to the correct entrance? If confusion reigns, it doesn't improve anyone's feeling of well-being or self-worth. (For your customers with physical disabilities, this is *even more important.* It's not enough to *have* an ADA-compliant entrance; customers need to be able to *find* it and get to it without intervening confusion.)

- *Do you use indecipherable company jargon that makes a customer feel stupid*—or, at the very least, like an outsider? Or do you translate your company-specific gobbledygook into language that makes your customers feel good about themselves because they can understand what you're saying?

- *Do you post signage with legalistic policy statements implying that you're expecting the worst of your customers:* signs and policies that are in reaction to the misdeeds of a small, or even hypothetical, group of misbehaving customers?

- Do employees make customers feel that they're an *interruption* of the employees' work rather than central to it, for example by continuing a conversation with a co-worker while a customer is trying to get their attention?

I'm sure you can think of additional junctures at which you're either making a customer feel good about themselves, or not. It's worth going through each of these. Because when customers feel good about themselves during their time with your business, they're going to feel better about your business as well.

## SMALL BUSINESS PROFILE: HELENE GODIN AND BY THE WAY BAKERY

As a girl, Helene Godin never had an Easy Bake oven, nor did this register as a deprivation. So she'd have been the last one to anticipate that one day she'd create a dominant chain of gluten-free bakeries in the Northeast, which is what her By the Way Bakery has become—growing to four retail locations so far and finding its way into sixty Whole Foods Markets and counting.

None of this would have happened if she didn't have two prominent traits in extreme doses, so extreme that you can almost* smell them on her:

First, what Godin calls "*my very broad, four-part definition of customer service . . .*

I. *Service to my neighbors,* who served me as well by being my muffin, brownie, and cupcake tasters (and later became my challah and rugelach tasters as well, as the Kosher market became a bigger share of our client base).**

2. *Service to my wonderful employees, vendors, and contractors,* without whom this work would feel too much like drudgery.

3. *Service to my retail customers,* no matter how small the sale.

---

\* Make that: actually.

\*\* In addition to being gluten-free and dairy-free, By the Way is kosher-certified. A kosher designation may not be a big draw where you live, but it goes a long way in New York. Besides, says Godin, "my Bubbie [grandmother] is kvelling [welling with pride] from above."

**Helene Godin in her By the Way Bakery**

*Photo by Julie Bidwell*

4. *Service to my big-ass customers as well"*—which, to her delight, now include those sixty Whole Foods Markets.

Second, a large dose of good-natured stubbornness and determination—"let's call it what it is, Micah. It's an utterly abnormal amount of chutzpah"—with zero understanding of "that's not possible," and a misunderstanding of the word "no," as in, "I don't think they really mean 'no'; I think they mean 'later.'"

## SHE SELLS AUDIBLE TO AMAZON, THEN TRIES (HALF-HEARTEDLY) TO RETIRE

Instead of dreaming as a child about a culinary future, from as far back as she can remember, her only goal was to be a lawyer. She was the very picture of a legal-minded Hermione Granger, even turning in an unsolicited legal brief in middle school to her astounded teacher, who happily gave her extra credit.

But after a twenty-two-year legal career, including stints as outside counsel for Columbia Records (later Sony Music), in-house counsel for *Reader's Digest* and NBC, and general counsel for Audible, where she and her team facilitated the sale of the audiobook company to Amazon, she settled into a post-lawyering retirement that lasted less than a week.

It only took four days for her to find herself, she tells me, "bored out of my skull." In an attempt to keep her sanity, this non-domestic goddess signed up for one of the only enrichment classes—"why not? I was bored"— she could find locally, which turned out to be "Vegan Baking Bootcamp."

She also took her first leisurely visit to a supermarket in years ("I hadn't done more than dash in and back out in years, practically with the engine running"), a trip that set her business antennae tingling; gluten-free products were getting what struck her as an inordinate—or, she started to think, *ordinate*—amount of shelf space in her local grocery.

However, as her plan to open a bakery began to form, "my family quickly offered the reasonable objection,

*'Helene, you don't know how to bake.'*

I said, 'I'll pick it up.'

*'But Mom, we've had to tell you for years that 'it's bake, not broil—charred muffins are not a thing.'*

Again, I told them,

*'I'll pick up the skills I'll need. And, by the way, it's going to be not just a bakery, but a gluten-free bakery. And not just a gluten-free bakery, but a gluten-free bakery where everything we'll offer will taste as good as, or better, than, products baked without ingredient constraints.'"*

## TURNING NEIGHBORS INTO CUSTOMERS BY INVOLVING THEM PRE-OPENING

This ambition was both easy to aspire to and fiendishly tricky to pull off; you can't just swap in one cup of gluten-free rice flour to replace one cup of wheat flour and expect to get the same results. "Gluten-free baking requires a blend, and I spent a long time playing with ratios to get that blend right, a flour mix that would work with the six core recipes I felt my bakery would need to be able to open: the blueberry muffin, the traditional brownie, the chocolate layer cake, and so forth."

Micah: "And you were doing all this where?"

Helene: "In my home kitchen.

"I created every recipe myself; I really threw myself into it. I had no training, but I was fearless. It was bake, bite, throw out. Bake, bite, throw out. Just keep doing it. Tweaking, learning as I go. Using myself and my neighbors as the tasters."

Micah: "Because your neighbors were going to be your core customers anyway."

Helene: "They were going to be my customers. Exactly! This is what I believe in: customer service to *everyone.* Even to people who aren't appropriate customers but don't know it yet. For example, we aren't nut-free, and if we tried that and failed, it would represent a potentially serious risk to those with allergies. So we are very upfront and very emphatic about making this clear and turning away the business."

## FINDING HER WAY INTO WHOLE FOODS

After getting her first By the Way Bakery up and running, in her quaint home town of Hastings-on-Hudson, where all those neighbors could in fact become daily customers, Godin quickly grew a new obsession: *finding her way into Whole Foods.*

She didn't have any plan for making this happen, beyond counting on her persistence and chutzpah to get her in. "I didn't know how these things worked; I just literally would pack up my stuff and bring it to the two Whole Foods stores nearest me, hoping to run into the right person. And, in fact, one day I did, because if you give anything enough time, it can work."

This initial contact resulted in an invitation to compete in a regional New Product Category Review (a bakeoff) in February of 2013, and soon Helene was happily having her products sold, on a small scale, at her local White Plains and Yonkers stores. This self-confessed "terrible driver" made most of the deliveries herself in her mini Cooper; when that proved too small, she graduated her delivery operation to a roomier Subaru. For two years, "life was good, because I had [Whole Foods] bragging rights, but I didn't need to worry about producing more than my tiny kitchen could handle."

## "THAT'S NICE OF YOU TO THINK OF ME, WHOLE FOODS . . . BUT CAN YOU CALL ME IN A YEAR?"

This gentle equilibrium collapsed in late 2014 when Helene got a call from a Whole Foods coordinator, Jay Jay, who announced with great fanfare that By the Way had been selected to supply baked goods to the new and massive Upper East Side store, which Whole Foods' calculations predicted would be one of the busiest in the country.

Helene's panicked response? "Call me in a year," once her little bakery had its ducks in a row. Jay Jay politely told her that this was a one-time offer, and implied, again politely, that she'd be crazy to not accept it. So, she took a deep breath, and at the end of that breath, heard herself say, "Of course!"

This invitation proved transformational. Not only did orders from the new Upper East Side store pour in, her By the Way products soon found their way into *all* of Whole Foods' Manhattan locations by fall of 2016 and outward into the surrounding states.

With the Subaru now obviously insufficient to handle deliveries, By the Way signed with a distributor in late 2018, allowing them to have their products reliably delivered to all the stores that required them.

## GIVING THANKS FOR CUSTOMERS— AND FOR THE CHANCE TO SERVE THEM

If you think Godin works every single day of the year, you'd be wrong. Some days of the year are Thanksgiving.[1]

"And, as I'm sitting down* at Thanksgiving, I'm able to picture all the people who sit down and eat things that I played a role in. And the idea that I brought some sweetness to their life makes me really happy."

## The Ideal, One-Word Review of Your Customer-Focused "Movie"

The type of experience—movie—you should be working to create will vary depending on the nature of your business. But if you're looking for a one-word review to summarize what a successful customer experience should feel like, "enchanting" is a good one to aim for. Enchantment comes when you transport a customer from the transactional and mundane to somewhere beyond. Think of how enchantment tends to power success in food and beverage (the restaurant industry), where the best operators have long understood that their jobs involve more than simply feeding guests. Here, enchantment can come in ways as simple as how Five Guys Burgers and Fries charms its customers (the nonallergic ones!) with throwback imagery of peanuts in brown bags. It's achieved at successful, if a tad kitschy, examples like Darden's ubiquitous Olive Garden, which strives to make the dining experience feel comfortably, vaguely "Italian" and to provide a destination and experience outside the ordinary for its customer base. And it includes the work of high-end restaurateurs like Jean-Georges Vongerichten, who can create experiences so immersive, so experiential, that a dinner can feel like an adventurous travel vacation to another country.

* I expect she means this metaphorically.

But enchantment can happen anywhere, even in the most serious of settings, such as the world-renowned Mayo Clinic. Headquartered in Rochester, Minnesota, with locations now across the country, Mayo has become a national and international destination for those with complicated conditions and serious prognoses. Alongside the legendary quality of the medicine, other elements that make the Mayo Clinic experience unique include the lighting (unlike the unnatural fluorescence favored by other hospitals, the lighting in Mayo facilities subtly warms the walls and incorporates outside light sources where possible), and a soundscape that is constructed with an emphasis on privacy and noise mitigation, with the hospital even specifying an extra layer of soundproofing in all of its latest building plans.[2]

Mayo Clinic makes other unusual choices that are intended to affect the way patients think about their experience there and their diagnoses. In one of these moves, the hospital has chosen to situate its children's cancer center right in the middle of one of its newer buildings (just off the lobby, in fact) as a statement that the institution isn't hiding from this oft-dreaded ailment, as it could feel if they were shunting the kids who suffer from it to a wing off a back corridor.

Thinking like this puts the patient—"the needs of the patient," as Mayo's motto puts it—at the center of the experience. Through all of the pain, fear, and uncertainty of a serious illness, this comfort and attention can be, in its own way, enchanting.

## REAL-LIFE MOMENTS FROM PATIENT EXPERIENCE CONSULTING: THE SQUEAKY CRASH CART AND THE POWER OF THE HALO EFFECT

Hospitals and other healthcare settings are, by and large, examples of "enforced hospitality"; customers (patients) come to the hospital because they need to, rather than on a lark. In these venues, there are multiple opportunities to make the experience better for patients and loved ones who—of course—don't need any more indignities heaped on them beyond those required by the actual medical procedures. To drive improvement in such settings, it's effective to look for little things that, if tweaked or mitigated, can create a "halo effect" on patient perceptions of their entire experience: specific improvements that can improve their overall impression.

Mitigating noise is an example. Noise is a source of stress for patients; it can cause sleeplessness (no kidding!) as well as increase heart rate and blood pressure. And it can also cause problems for the noisy institution itself when the noise drives a patient to give negative ratings on patient satisfaction surveys (called **HCAHPS**).

Remediating noise requires a concerted effort on multiple fronts: fix that doggone squeaky wheel on a noisy cart; post "Use Your Inside Voice" or "Patients Sleeping" signs for staff; rethink supply deliveries and shift-change routines. And consider following the lead of hospitals that have made progress on the issue by installing a system of lights at the nurses' station: when the noise level rises, a light flashes red and an alarm chimes—softly. (And, when it's time to renovate your hospital building, I suggest advocating for fundamental improvements such as walls that continue *above* the acoustical tile drop ceiling, so that sound is no longer allowed to pass right into a patient's room from neighboring spaces.)

It may seem like reducing noise levels is a limited kind of win, but *the concept of the halo effect is an important one.* When the patient experience is improved in *one* area (like noise) it tends to *spark higher customer experience ratings overall*, even in areas that haven't yet been addressed by the organization.

## The Hazards of Stagnation

In general, humans can adapt to most any situation, good or bad, over time, returning eventually to their baseline level of happiness after the shock, positive or negative, of the change in the situation wears off. In psychology, this is called the principle of *hedonic adaptation*:

what's bad will eventually seem less bad (which is handy), but what's good will eventually seem less positive as well (which can be a drag).

Hedonic adaptation is a force to be reckoned with when you're trying to maintain customer interest and engagement. It means that once you've succeeded in engaging—and, ideally, enchanting—a customer, you may need to work at *keeping* that customer happy and engaged.

Keeping it fresh isn't easy. Any initially meaningful element of your customer experience can grow stale over time. What's fabulous to a customer on a first visit may seem like "fine, but nothing new" on the fifth. In apparel retailing, at one time was a fresh idea to add a flourish at the end of each sale by having the sales associate step around the counter to the customer's side to hand over the shopping bag. Truly a lovely idea, but one that can look a bit stagey after customers see it too many times. Similarly, it was once the rage among white tablecloth restaurants to print the dining guest's name or business logo on their copy of the evening's menu (this was back when putting your color inkjet through its paces was the latest thing). The first time that customers encountered this gesture, they were likely impressed. But when the restaurant tried the same trick again on a third or fourth visit, customers tended to greet the gesture with, at best, a yawn.

There can be a shelf life for such choreographed service practices, and you'll ideally change them up before they start to wear on your customers. Your customers are dynamic, aware people, and the experience offered by your establishment needs to reflect this.

But remember: *the goal of customer service and the customer experience isn't buzz; it's loyalty,* which means that *change for change's sake isn't inherently positive.* There's always the hazard of removing elements that returning customers still value and are likely to miss. Though customers do seek some innovation and freshness from companies they give their money to, if a company invests *only* in change, how can it ask a customer to remain loyal? (What, after all, is left for them to be loyal *to?*)

There's an inherent tension between innovation and tradition, and it's hard to get the mix right, to update the customer experience without changing your brand's essential nature. "Cultivating loyalty is a tricky business," says Patrick O'Connell, whose Inn at Little Washington has developed and sustained avid customer loyalty for more than forty years so far, a rare feat for an independent restaurateur and innkeeper. "It requires maintaining a rigorous level of consistency while constantly adding newness and a little surprise—freshening the guest experience without changing its core identity."

## Money Can Break the Spell of Enchantment, But It Doesn't Need To

*Charging what you're worth isn't what breaks the spell of enchantment.* In fact, for many customers a high, or at least solid, price, in exchange for great service and a great experience, can figure in as part of the enchantment. However, there *are* ways that money can break the spell and sabotage an otherwise-enchanting experience. For starters, no customer, no matter how well-heeled, likes to be hit with nickel-and-dime charges such as fees for Wi-Fi. Or gotcha-priced $9 bottles of Evian in a hotel room. (Or, for that matter, a punitive add-on charge if you want additional sauces for your McNuggets, as the angrily scribbled sign at a drive-through near my home demanded.)

It's not the cost involved that's so offensive, at least not *exactly*. It's that you're interrupting the customer experience and the customer–provider relationship with mercantile, even mercenary, behavior. This can quickly undo the enchantment that you've worked hard to bring about.

There are multiple money-related ways to break the spell of enchantment, and it's important to stay on guard against these as you do business. These include aggressive billing practices; the very language you use to talk about money, like bluntly saying "you owe" to a customer, rather than "our records show a balance"; tricky or unfair return and refund policies; and more.

Thoughtful operators of every kind of business know that pricing matters. Not solely the absolute price itself (whether it's high, low, or someplace in between) but also *how* the price is presented. In retail, a good example in this regard is Warby Parker, the wildly successful eyeglass purveyor, which has been successful at keeping money from breaking the enchantment of its customer experience. Prices are posted in small but readable type. They're quoted in round numbers ($95, not $94.99). The return and exchange program is simple and generous, thus reducing the money-related tension of a purchase (thirty days to return or exchange your purchase; a year to get a replacement if you scratch them). And—and this is a master touch—in spite of the small amount of space available in their compact and highly profitable stores, shelf space is visibly "wasted" on books and other slower-moving but attractive items. Not because these items are big sellers, but because *their presence suggests that this enterprise is about more than money.*

Every business, and every customer base, is unique, and the pricing approach that's right for your business is going to be unique as well. But whatever your business context, pursuing *the goal of removing money as a stress point* is important if you want to keep your customers safely nestled in the enchantment zone.

## CUSTOMER SERVICE FOR HIGH NET WORTH INDIVIDUALS (HNWIs): WHERE MONEY MATTERS LESS, OR AT LEAST MATTERS DIFFERENTLY

Within a variety of industries—financial services, banking, insurance, travel, retail, luxury hospitality, and more—you'll find companies that either devote themselves entirely to, or have set up a division to specialize in serving, the well-to-do, or, as they're known in the lingo of this world, "high net worth individuals" (HNWIs). The kind of customer service, or client service, if you prefer, required for high net worth individuals is *broadly* similar to what's required to provide customer service and support to the general consumer population, but (and, as Pee-wee Herman would say, it's a "big but") there are subtle differences and intensifiers. Here are the four factors that I stress to my client companies that specialize in serving HNWIs, as most likely to trip them up—and as most important to get just right.

- **Elevated customer service expectations due to the high customer service norms encountered elsewhere in an HNWI's personal and consumer lives.** The benchmarks against which an HNWI measures customer service are generally higher than they would be for another consumer, thus making the challenge of providing great client service both that much harder and that much more essential.

- **The likely disconnection between your customers' lifestyle frame of reference and that of your employees.** The economic and lifestyle realities of high net worth customers may be light-years removed from those of your employees, causing an empathy and practicality gap in service conversations and recommendations. Ross Buchmueller, CEO of the PURE Group of Insurance Companies, which serves affluent homeowners and families, recalls overhearing an employee at a company (not *his* company, by the way) telling a high net worth client that, "I'd never recommend anyone taking a $10,000 deductible, because I could never afford to pay that much myself if something went wrong," which, while a candid comment—and certainly valid within the employee's own worldview—was not necessarily good advice for a client who could easily self-insure for that amount or more, and for whom it might have been a big moneysaver on premiums and a smart financial move.

- **A lower valuation placed on modest sums of money.** The value equation (Value = Personal Benefit - Cost and Inconvenience) is likely to be calculated differently by a high net worth customer, with less concern for cost and more value placed on reducing inconvenience and maximizing nonfinancial personal benefit.

■ A need, among HNWIs, for reassurance that they're not being taken advantage of. HNWIs don't necessarily mind spending more to get more. *But they do get leery of being taken advantage of, since they know they make an appealing and potentially easy target.* Reassurance—taking pains to avoid making the client feel stupid or like a mark who's being hustled—goes a long way here.

## TRAINING CLIENT SERVICE REPRESENTATIVES TO SERVE A HNWI CLIENT POPULATION

When training employees who will be providing customer service to high net worth customers, it's important those employees receive specific HNWI-focused training that addresses the issues I've brought up here, so that employees will be sensitive to what is likely to be different in HNWI expectations and desires.

## WHEN THINGS GO WRONG FOR HNWI CLIENTS

Extraordinary customer service is, of course, of utmost importance when things go wrong for any customer of any socioeconomic rank, but how an HNWI client will, implicitly, define "extraordinary" can be distinct in nuanced ways, due to their wealth and lifestyle. In the example of insurance losses, "the normal calculation of what insurance owes a client could be stated as, 'we repay what is fair when called on to do so,'" says Buchmueller, the PURE Group of Insurance Companies' CEO. "But what a loss means to *anyone*, and perhaps to a high net worth individual in particular, is more than a monetary loss that can be compensated for by receiving a check."

The general principle to follow here is to *always consider the nonmonetary part of the loss calculation*: To take the example of trying to help a displaced insurance client secure temporary replacement housing, this would mean looking at more than square footage, appliances, and finishes and to also consider calculations such as commuting distance and neighborhood, with an eye toward replicating the client's pre-loss situation as closely as possible.

Or, consider this actual example from the PURE Group of Insurance Companies, whose client family had an extraordinary collection of Christmas tree ornaments destroyed in a home fire. The PURE staff, taking the attitude that "we want to help make our clients whole again," went to work with independent vendors and auction houses, as well as scouring eBay, and managed to replace the entire collection in time for Christmas.

# READER'S CHEATSHEET
# FOR CHAPTER 5

**The importance of creating an experience:** With all the emphasis in business today on streamlining and efficiency (which *are* important), be sure that you don't neglect an important part of the customer experience: the actual experiential aspect.

**Make it cinematic:** Think of creating a customer experience as similar to creating a movie for the benefit of your customers. Let customers benefit from your attention to cinematic details and give your customers a chance to get caught up in the emotions and storyline of the experience.

**Strive for enchantment:** If you're looking for one word that summarizes what a successful customer experience should feel like in most industries and contexts, "enchanting" is a good one to aim for. *Enchantment comes when you transport a customer somewhere beyond the transactional and the mundane.*

**Don't risk breaking the spell of enchantment through awkwardly handled touchpoints:** Every touchpoint that occurs during the customer's time with you bears the risk of breaking the spell of enchantment, if it's handled poorly—that is, abruptly, inconsiderately, or awkwardly.

**In particular, take a look at how you handle matters of, and discussions of, money.** Nickel and diming, using the wrong language to discuss money, and overly insistent billing practices are all money-related gaffes that can disrupt your customers' enchantment.

**The hazards of staleness—and, conversely, of change for change's sake:** In psychology, the principle of *hedonic adaptation* suggests that humans can adapt to almost any situation, good or bad, over time. Hedonic adaptation can be a challenge when you're working to maintain customer interest and engagement: Once you've succeeded in engaging—and, ideally, enchanting—a customer, you may need to work at *keeping* them engaged and happy by adding or revising "points in the plotline."

But change for change's sake isn't inherently positive. There's always the hazard of removing elements that returning customers still value and are likely to miss. *It takes work to get the mix right between innovation and tradition.*

1. One way to think of the customer experience is as a movie put on for the benefit of customers. Whether or not we use this metaphor in our organization, do we pay sufficient attention to pacing, staging, lighting, and other soft, dramatic details of the customer experience? Would there be value for us in doing so?

2. This chapter suggests that, in most industries, a good customer experience theme to aim for is "enchantment." In our organization, do we strive to enchant our customers, alongside the more traditional goals of efficiency, reducing friction and the like? If not, should we?

3. Mishandling issues, including language, related to money can be an easy way to break the spell of enchantment. Have we looked at issues related to money from this emotional angle? Would it be worthwhile to do so?

4. Micah suggests that we should look at our customer experience with an eye toward *making customers feel good about themselves*. Some of the ways organizations fail to do this that he mentions are confusing signage and poor instructions, use of internal jargon with external customers, and obstructions or unclear directions for customers with disabilities. Do we spend enough time in our organization looking at the

experience we provide from the angle of how it makes customers feel about themselves? Would there be value in giving
this concept more consideration?

Reminder: All of the reading group guides are available as a single
document you can download for free at **guides.micahsolomon.com**.

# DIVERSITY AND INCLUSION NOTES FOR CHAPTER 5

FROM JAN JONES BLACKHURST, CAESARS INTERNATIONAL BOARD OF DIRECTORS, FORMER CAESARS VICE PRESIDENT FOR PUBLIC POLICY AND CORPORATE RESPONSIBILITY (AND THE FIRST FEMALE MAYOR OF LAS VEGAS)

Creating an *inclusive customer experience* (ensuring that the experience you provide is comfortable for diverse guests and that service delivery is equitable for all) is a goal that all of us who serve customers need to aspire to and work, relentlessly, to bring about.

The first step in creating such an experience is to ensure that the process used to select the employees who will be creating the experience is inclusive, right down to the words you use to *describe* the position for which you are hiring. Studies show that if you change the way you write a job description to make it more inclusive—e.g., to make it more feminine in a traditionally male field—*it increases the number of applicants overall*, not just among, in this case, female applicants. Then, once you have those applicants, ensure that the screening and interviewing processes are as demographically blind as possible, and work similarly on diversifying the advancement opportunities on offer.

Similar steps can be taken to describe your product/service offering as more inclusive as well, including in such areas as gender, race, ethnicity, sexual orientation, physical and nonphysical disability, age, religion, socioeconomic factors, and more.

Beyond this, it's essential that your employees walk the walk once the newly courted demographic of customers arrives! Sending out promotions to get more same-sex couples to come to hotels or doing the same for African American businesspeople, for example, is great. But it only works if your associates are just as welcoming once the new guests are on-property. Training and managing employees to provide a welcoming environment for all is an essential endeavor that needs to be pursued on an ongoing basis. Until team members' reactions to, say, a nontraditional family with two moms is on a par with their reaction to a heterosexual couple, it's essential to keep trying. And then try some more.

# BUILDING A BACKBONE TO SUPPORT THE SMILES

Although simple dumb luck *might* allow you to impress a customer *now and again*, it's not the way to go about achieving customer service excellence that's consistent and can be relied upon. This requires putting in place the standards and systems that can enable you to create repeatable results across a variety of situations and with a changing cast of employees. In this chapter, I'll first talk about the comparatively simple concept of *standards*, then move on to customer service *systems*—a closely related but somewhat more involved concept.

A *standard* can be anything from a tactic for performing a task more easily and successfully (an auto repair shop could have a standard for how to put a lug nut securely on a wheel without overtightening) to a brand-consistency standard (the same repair shop could have a standard for which magazine titles to have in its customer lounge: "Go easy on the *Monster Trucks* and *Gearhead* magazines, please. And if you ever are considering 'donating' your personal copies of *Maxim* to the customer lounge, we have a Performance Improvement Plan waiting just for you!")

Some standards can be quite specific. When you order a caramel macchiato at Starbucks, your drink is finished with a precise pattern of caramel sauce: seven vertical lines crossed with seven horizontal lines which are then topped with two full circles around the crosshatching just created. This standard provides more than visual consistency; it all but ensures a small amount of caramel sauce in almost every sip. This is true regardless of which Starbucks location (they've just topped 30,000 as I type this) you're sitting in when you take those sugar-laced sips. And those wooden stir sticks? A Starbucks standard specifies that they be sourced from a particular variety of birch tree that company testing has shown won't interact with the flavor of a coffee drink. Also, in keeping with the company's environmental goals, a separate environmental sourcing standard calls for these birch trees to be grown on a sustainable farm, where they can do double duty by shading the coffee plants grown below them.

A service *system* is typically more elaborate than a service standard. It's any set of actions that a business executes consistently to make the experience better—that is, warmer, faster, safer, easier, or more engaging—for its customers.

To get a handle on this, it helps to divide service systems into the following categories:

> *Preparatory systems* help clear the way for a great service experience *prior* to its delivery.

> *Execution systems* help employees *during* customer interactions and enable them to consistently provide a high level of service.

> *Customer preference and experience tracking systems* enhance the customer experience by making it more personally appropriate to the particular customer being served.

*Continuous improvement systems* are intended to make *future* service encounters even better.

Finally, *service recovery systems* are for handling the situation when things go wrong.

Let's look at these one by one:

**Preparatory systems** involve a variety of behind-the-scenes disciplines, including engineering, finance and accounting, shipping and receiving, purchasing, employee training, and HR. Your daily Customer Service Minute (see chapter 3) falls into this category as well.

**Execution systems** are customer service systems that kick in during the course of the live customer experience, where they're integral to delivering superior service. Although some of these systems are dependent on technology, it's often the nontechnical systems that save the day by helping employees do their best work.

To return to Starbucks, not only does the company have precise standards for the amount of the ingredient (syrup, sauce, or add-in) to be put into different beverages, the company also ensures that these precise standards are met, day in and day out, without requiring endless training or extraordinary feats of memory. The company pulls this off via a simple-to-use system: Instead of requiring baristas to memorize a long list of formulas, Starbucks has created a set of color-coded pumps and spoons, each of which is paired with a particular ingredient to ensure that the correct amount can be easily and accurately dispensed. The barista just has to follow a simple procedure that is identical regardless of the syrup, sauce, or add-in in question: Three pumps of the ingredient go into a tall drink (for the uninitiated: "tall" is the ironic name given to the smallest drink size at Starbucks), four go into a grande, and five into a venti.

Some execution systems are designed to provide a single aspect of customer service delivery, such as ensuring that customers are acknowledged and made to feel welcome. One such execution system is the 10-5-3 sequence. This widely used system has proven its utility in a broad range of settings, from retail bank branches to hotels to cruise ships. Because of its wide usage, there are multiple variations of the 10-5-3 system in existence. The one I favor is employed by Jeroen Quint, the general manager of Hotel Irvine in Orange County, California. At Jeroen's hotel, every employee is instructed to use the 10-5-3 system whenever they encounter a guest, as follows:

> **At 10 feet:** Look up from what you are doing and acknowledge the guest with direct eye contact and a nod.
> **At 5 feet:** Smile, with your lips and eyes.
> **At 3 feet**[*]**:** Verbally greet the guest and offer a time-of-day greeting ("Good morning"). Use a tone of voice appropriate to your work area or where you encounter the guest.

**Customer preference and experience tracking systems** can be a powerful way to improve the customer experience. One such system is employed at John Meadow's LDV Hospitality, which operates more than twenty restaurants; its brands include Scarpetta, American Cut, Dolce Italian, and others. In each of LDV's restaurants, customers' dining preferences are kept on file. This is accomplished with the assistance of servers, managers, and hosts who make note of patrons' preferences, perhaps for a particular wine or cocktail, or for a meat temperature, and enter those details into the diners' profiles. These are compiled in a database that is linked across all LDV properties, regardless of brand. For example, if you're a regular at Scarpetta and you favor a particular martini, that would be flagged in the system so that when you visit The Regent Cocktail

---

* If the smile wasn't reciprocated at 5 feet or if it otherwise feels that you will be interrupting—if the guest is absorbed with their cell phone, for example—do not proceed with the "3 feet" part of this sequence.

Club in Miami, the drink will be ready for you upon arrival. (It's important to note that LDV Hospitality employees are expected to be scrupulous about keeping such technological enhancements *out of view* of the customer, integrating them with human-delivered service as invisibly as possible, so that the resulting service flourishes seem magical rather than mechanical or rote.)

Tracking the experience of your customers *while they are still experiencing your service* is a master touch you may consider adding to your repertoire. If you put a system in place that alerts you to service glitches that arise in the course of a customer's visit, it will allow you to follow up later in the same visit to ensure that all was handled and that your customer feels well cared for. For example, if a guest encounters a problem early in their visit to a spa, resort, or hotel, the shortcoming should be addressed *immediately,* of course. But also, ideally, *later* in the course of their visit the guest will be greeted by a manager who will say something along the lines of, "I understand there was a challenge early on in your time with us, so I want to follow up and see how things are going and whether I can be of further assistance." This is more sensitive than a know-nothing follow-up like, "How's everything going—great?"

A new development along these lines that is growing in popularity, particularly in contact centers, is real-time "sentiment monitoring" based on all channels of customer interaction. This can be a powerful tool, as it offers the customer support agent an immediate view of the customer's current level of satisfaction, as determined by an automated scan of all recent correspondence and interactions, so that the agent can determine appropriate actions to take. Real time sentiment monitoring is now built into some customer support platforms, such as NextOS from Nextiva (see the sidebar in chapter 8).

**Continuous improvement systems** allow an organization to identify flaws and to improve itself over time by correcting them. In such a setup, employees are empowered (and perhaps required) to identify and log flaws they come across that are detracting from the customer experience.

Some of these systems are quite involved, and their effectiveness is well established. For example, the *lean* approach (also referred to as *lean manufacturing* and, historically, as the *Toyota Production System*) is an organizational philosophy and methodology that is well worth studying in depth (see following sidebar). If you aren't ready for such a comprehensive undertaking, baby steps can also make a difference; there are many ways to set up a continuous improvement system on a more limited scale at your company. Even the lowly suggestion box qualifies as a continuous improvement system if the suggestions received are systematically logged and then considered for appropriate action.

## AN AFRICAN AMERICAN–FOCUSED BLOWOUT BAR GOES ALL IN ON LEAN MANUFACTURING METHODOLOGY

Paralee Boyd is a Detroit-based salon geared toward African American women, a demographic that the major blowout bars have been slow to cater to. After Paralee Boyd's founder, Dana White, bootstrapped her business with $30,000 in personal capital, she took the unusual move of going all-in on lean (a.k.a. lean manufacturing) methodology in designing, equipping, and operating the salon. As Tanya Klich writes in Forbes.com, White made use of her Detroit connections by bringing in engineers from GM and Ford. "The engineers told me," Klich quotes her as saying, that "we can show you where to place salon seats, towels, and hairstyling tools to speed up the services" by eliminating the types of waste that lean methodology counsels against, include *waiting*, *motion*, and *nonutilized talent*.

The efficiency of White's salon, including the speed with which it can get clients in and out, has allowed Paralee Boyd to grow rapidly, without resorting to advertising, notes Klich, as well as boosting the earning potential for salon employees, who are both paid an above-minimum wage and are eligible for tips for every styling they undertake.

**Service recovery systems** kick in when your company, your customers, or some uncontrollable force like the weather introduces a wrinkle into the service experience you were intending to provide. A great service organization will recognize these inevitabilities and establish systems ahead of time for handling a variety of predictable service calamities, providing clearly defined solutions for each. Such systems allow your employees to serve customers in the best possible way in the face of particular types of stressors that your business is likely to encounter.

The entire staff should be trained on these prepackaged remedies; having these fixes in place and rehearsed ahead of time allows employees to handle common problems with ease and grace. For example, if you're in the restaurant business, it's only a matter of time before an employee spills a drink on one of your guests, a waiter rings in the wrong order, a chef cooks a steak to the wrong temperature, or the cork in a bottle of wine turns out to be spoiled. Because these situations are predictable and recurring, a response sequence can be prepared ahead of time, ready to be implemented when the inevitable comes about.

When these fixes go above and beyond customer expectations, it can turn the resolution of such glitches into opportunities to generate deep customer loyalty and powerful word of mouth. When a guest spills a glass of red wine in the spectacular and intimate dining room of The Inn at Little Washington, making a mess of the linen tabletop and causing distress and embarrassment among the diners, something remarkable happens. The *entire* service staff stops whatever they are doing, practically in midmotion, and hurries over to help refresh and reset the table. Two staff members clear the table, while another fetches and spreads a new tablecloth. Two other employees place an entirely new set of dishes and glassware on the table, while the sommelier replaces the glass of wine. The food is refreshed or replated in the kitchen and, once all of this has been accomplished, the flowers are placed back on the table. The Inn calls this an "emergency clear" and uses this response procedure to transform what could have been a protracted and awkward period of mess and confusion into a two-minute flurry of choreographed activity that leaves guests open-mouthed in awe.

Unfortunately, prepackaged fixes can't cover everything, because not every mishap and not every customer reaction to a mishap can be predicted in advance. This makes it essential that you develop a *general customer service recovery framework* that can be used for those times when the situation hits the fan, and the customer hits the roof.

Having a service recovery framework is important because, even in the best of times, it's hard for most of us to improvise entirely from scratch without a structure to guide us and upon which to fall back. And a situation that calls for service recovery is, by definition, far from the best of times. When things haven't gone smoothly and a customer is upset, employees are likely to feel embarrassed, or defensive, or put-upon, or angry—or all of these at once. With so much emotion flying around, it's hard for even the most seasoned and even-tempered customer service professionals to do their best.

If your organization hasn't already committed to a different service recovery system, let me offer you my own four-step MAMA (the acronym's in tribute to the Italian Mama, whom you'll meet in a moment) service recovery framework. I expect it will stand you in good stead.

## A RESOURCE FOR MY READERS

If you'd like a standalone, printable copy of the four-step MAMA™ service recovery approach, let me know by email at mama@micahsolomon.com.

## The MAMA™ Method for Customer Service Recovery

Here are the four steps to take when responding to a service failure:

**M**ake time to listen

**A**cknowledge and apologize

(Have a) **M**eeting of minds

**A**ct! and follow up

### MAKE TIME TO LISTEN

- Immediately stop whatever you're doing.
- Listen with your ears, your eyes, and your body. Don't interrupt the customer with questions or explanations.
- Only *after* listening quietly, strive to learn more about the situation by probing for what the customer is *specifically* upset about.

### ACKNOWLEDGE AND APOLOGIZE

- Acknowledge the situation and, if called for (by which I mean the customer feels an apology is warranted, not necessarily that you do), apologize sincerely.
- Even if you have no reason to feel that you're at fault, you should convey to the customer that you recognize and regret what they've gone through.
- Be sure to make it a real apology and not a fakey-fake apology, like "I'm sorry if you feel that way." (Delivering a bogus apology like this, through gritted teeth, is probably worse than not apologizing and all.)

### (HAVE A) MEETING OF MINDS

- Align yourself with the customer's expectations for what a solution would look like. Determine what would be acceptable to them and practical (or even possible) for you to make happen. (Include your customer in the process and remain open to a different vision of a successful solution emerging at this point.)

- Once you have a match, spell out the agreed-on solution, as you understand it.
- Commit to exactly what you will do to resolve the issue and by when.

ACT! AND FOLLOW UP
- Take care of the issue as promised.
- Follow up with anyone to whom you've assigned all or part of the resolution.
- Follow up with the customer to ensure all is well.
- Later on, examine what went wrong with an eye toward identifying negative patterns, systemic issues, and choke-points (for example, *repeated* complaints of long lines on Tuesday afternoons or of a website that loads slowly, but only on weekend nights), and strive to learn from the error, using this new knowledge, where applicable, to refine future company operations and training.

## WHEN RESPONDING TO AN UPSET CUSTOMER, CHANNEL YOUR INNER ITALIAN MAMA

If you're face to face—or phone to phone or terminal to terminal—with a customer who's upset, a customer to whom something bad (in their opinion) has happened, consider putting the archetype of an adoring Italian mother to work for you. She's the spirited, if over the top, model I've been proposing for customer service recovery ever since she was introduced in my first book, *Exceptional Service, Exceptional Profit*, coauthored by the luminary Leonardo Inghilleri (who, himself, is as Italian as they come) and me.

Here's how this hypothetical, doting, parent might respond after her child takes a tumble:

*Oh, my darling, look at what happened! Oh, you skinned your knee on that walkway, my bambino; let me kiss that terrible wound. Shall we watch a little TV? And here's a lollipop for you while I bandage you up!*

Minus the baby talk, this Italian mother is a great model for how to react to service failures. While it's very much an exaggeration, the exaggeration is intended to make the following point clear: that it works much better to express your empathy to an upset customer than to take the more typical approach, which we might call the Courtroom Method:

*Let's sort out the facts of the situation. Were you wearing proper protective clothing per the sidewalk user's manual at the time your knee impacted the concrete? And I need to ask, young fellow: Were you exceeding the sidewalk speed limit?*

To repeat: This is an exaggeration to make a point. But the point is extremely important if you want to succeed in working with upset customers: Before you rush to solve a problem—or, worse, to assign blame—take a moment to acknowledge that the customer is upset and feels wronged.[1]

## Failures Result from Broken Systems

When the customer experience at your business goes south, it's often because one or more of your systems are broken or haven't been set up in the first place. Let's say you own a body shop. A customer complains (in person, if you're lucky; on Yelp, if you're not) about a disappointing early morning interaction with one of your cashiers. Your first impulse may be to bite the cashier's head off, but I hope that you'll hold that impulse, and your teeth, in check and look at the situation dispassionately.

If you have the chance to study the performance of your cashier, you'll likely discover a set of problems that runs something like this: they're not well organized; their computer's not booted up by the start of her shift—in time to serve the first customer who walks up; there's no pen close at hand so that customers can sign the charge slips; and so forth.

Even though each of these failures starts with a personal pronoun, what you actually have is a failure of systems, including some or all of the following:

- **Training and preparation.** Shouldn't the cashier have been prepped on the necessary supplies and the login procedure for starting a shift? Going deeper than this, has your cashier been introduced to and coached in an effective workplace organization system—perhaps 5S, which is the workspace-organization aspect of lean methodology?

- **Scheduling.** Because you were pinching payroll pennies, was your cashier told to show up at work the very minute the shift began rather than a more realistic fifteen or twenty minutes earlier, which would have allowed the cashier to mentally settle in, get the bank ready to make change, find a pen, organize the workplace, boot up the computers, and so forth?

- **Employee selection (hiring).** Saying "there was a failure in hiring" is a bit different from saying "it's the employee's fault." If the cashier isn't a good fit for the position—if they're not detail-oriented enough, for example—it's not the cashier's fault; it's the fault of the system that was responsible for selecting the cashier, and it's time to get to work improving that system.

## When a Problem Happens More than Once

A rule of thumb is that when something goes wrong *once*, it might be a particular employee's fault, or it could be just a fluke. If it happens *twice*, though, you should begin to suspect that it's the fault of a broken or missing system. When you encounter repeated, identical mistakes, the smart move is to look at the system involved: to review its design and how it is, or isn't, being implemented.

Overall, your ability to discover the systems in your company that are poorly designed, imperfectly implemented and maintained, or flat-out missing depends on having built a culture where mistakes are embraced as learning opportunities, and customer complaints are seen as opportunities for improvement. If you do the opposite—if you react to every issue that comes up by instigating a witch hunt—*you'll drive your employees to focus on covering up their mistakes rather than on solving problems and providing superior service.* Employees need to be comfortable admitting when they've slipped up so that such slips can be fixed for the sake of future performance—systematically.

## TO WIN OVER COMPLAINERS, MODEL YOURSELF ON THE "BRANSON CURRY METHOD"

"A complaint is a chance to turn a customer into a lifelong friend," says Richard Branson. "I say that seriously, not as some press release baloney. At Virgin, we really think that if we address a complaint well, and even involve the customer in the solution, it brings customers closer to our brand." In other words, while* a systematic approach to customer service recovery is essential, the right *mindset* can go a long way: an attitude of openness, of receiving each complaint as a gift and opportunity rather than as an intrusion or assault.

My favorite Virgin-related example of this approach: A passenger in Virgin Atlantic's first-class cabin (which Virgin brilliantly refers to as "upper class") once sent Branson a devastating, though hilarious, culinary critique of a curry dish that the passenger had the misfortune of encountering on a Mumbai-to-Heathrow flight. The passenger's letter included many memorable lines, such as describing one item on his tray as a "miscellaneous . . . cuboid of beige matter" and explaining elsewhere that, "the potato masher had obviously broken, and so it was decided the next best thing would be to pass the potatoes through the digestive tract of a bird." What's most instructive about the story, though, isn't the pointed prose of

---

* Or "whilst," as Sir Richard would be more likely to put it.

the complaint, but how Branson responded: not with defensiveness, but by *inviting the passenger to help Virgin Atlantic improve its menu by serving on Virgin Atlantic's advisory board for food.*

## A System for Customer-Friendly Language

When I undertake a customer service initiative, I typically develop, for my client company, a simple system—really, just a phrasebook—of words and phrases to avoid when interacting with customers, each one paired with a preferable alternative or alternatives. This phrasebook will come to serve as a guide that employees can refer to and to which they can hold themselves accountable.

Although you don't want to *over*-prescribe the content of employee communication, you shouldn't abdicate your responsibility for what comes out of employees' mouths either. Although I encourage companies to avoid stilted, formalistic communications, I also encourage them to provide language guidance to employees, with an eye (or, I should say, an ear) toward making life as pleasant as it can be for customers.

Here are a few examples:

> **1. Discouraged:**
> *"You need to . . ."*
> For example:
> "You *need to* come back at 11:00, when we're open."
> "You *need to* fill out this form."
> "You *need to* provide me with an imprint of your credit card."
> **Preferred:**
> "We'll be ready to serve you at 11:00."
> "May I ask you to fill out our health history form before we start your massage?"
> "May I trouble you for an imprint of your credit card?"

These recommended responses vary based on the situation, but they all avoid the formulation of telling a customer that they "need" to do something. When you tell a customer "You need to . . . ," it can lead to resentment, causing the customer to think, "I don't *need* to do anything, buddy—I'm your customer!" Of course, at times customers *do* need to do things (pay their bills, show proper ID, and so forth). But there are ways to get this point across to all but the most ornery customers without bossily ordering them around.

## 2. Discouraged:

*"Like I said . . ."* (Also, *"Again . . ."*)

**Preferred:**

Simply *repeat what you said* or find a better way to explain it.

When you tell a customer, "*Like I said*, Mrs. Smith, we will be closed on Thursdays from noon to 3:00 p.m.," it conveys to Mrs. Smith that she hasn't been listening as well as you feel she should be.

*As professionals serving customers, it's our job to convey information, not to judge our customers' attentiveness and comprehension skills.* So, as required, repeat yourself. And, if necessary, repeat yourself yet again.

## 3. Discouraged:

*"To be honest with you . . ."* (Also, *"To be perfectly frank . . ."*)

**Preferred:**

There's no need for a replacement for this phrase; just stop saying it!

Think about what "to be honest with you" conveys to a customer: If you say, "To be honest with you, Mr. Johnson," what were you doing *before* that moment in your conversation with Mr. Johnson—lying through your teeth?

**4. Discouraged:**

*"You owe us _____."*

**Preferred:**

*"Our records show a balance of _____."*

Certainly, customers *are* going to owe you money, and when they do, you deserve to get paid. But it's generally better to talk obliquely about money that's owed, rather than directly. While "Your balance is," "Our records indicate a balance," and so on (the proper wording is often industry-specific) are all fine, but a blunt, "You owe us $____" is never going to work. It may get you paid, but it isn't going to make a customer feel good about the interaction.

**5. Discouraged:**

*"Please hold."*

**Preferred:**

"May* I place you on a brief hold?"

It's important to customers who are calling to know they have a *choice* of whether to hold or not. Most customers, if given a choice, will agree to a brief hold, but only if they know the choice is theirs. This way they can feel confident that the one hypothetical time they may call in the future when they really *can't* hold, you aren't going to force them to do so.

**6. Discouraged [in response to a customer thanking an employee]:**

*"No problem."*

---

\* I'm not going to dive into the "may I" vs. "can I" morass, other than to say that, to some customers (English teachers in particular), "can I" will grate on their ears, yet to others, "may I" will sound like you're putting on airs as if you wish you were working in Buckingham Palace.

**Preferred:**
*"You're welcome."*
*"My pleasure."*
*"[I'm] glad I could help."*

The problems with "no problem" (as a reply to an expression of thanks from a customer) are legion. First off, *your customer invested their effort in thanking you,* and you're being dismissive of this effort. Second, you're implying that whatever they required you to do for them could, potentially, have been a problem. Finally, why bring the word "problem" into the mix at all, even if it's modified by that little "no"?

Having said this, *"no problem" is not the hill you want to die on. If you have a great employee who simply will not stop saying, "no problem" (or even "no worries"), perhaps they know their specific customer better than you do.*

## REAL-LIFE MOMENTS IN CUSTOMER SERVICE TRAINING

One of the various problems with the phrase "no problem" is that it's hard to stop customers from thinking about a problem once you suggest the idea of "problem" in the first place. In order to make this point, I'll sometimes ask participants in my training sessions and customer service workshops to . . .

*"Be sure not to think about a big, pink elephant!"*

Then, I'll ask participants what they're thinking about, and invariably, they'll call out,

*"A big, pink elephant!"*

(Make that *almost* invariably. One woman blurted out,

*"French fries!"*

. . . which I certainly respect as an equally valid response.)

Here are a few other less-than-thoughtful phrases that are likely to leave a poor impression:

- **"Young lady" or "young man" (to an elderly woman or man).** What could be more thoughtless than when, say, a TSA agent tells a woman of obviously advancing age, "Young lady, step right through the scanner"? She already knows she's no longer young; why take this opportunity to remind her?
- **"There are *two wheelchairs* on this plane" (meaning that there are *two passengers with disabilities* on the plane).** Passengers with disabilities are humans. They are not pieces of equipment; they are not "wheelchairs." Yet you'll hear flight attendants remark to each other or to crew on the ground that "We have two wheelchairs on this plane" or "We're clear—we don't have any wheelchairs on this plane."
- **"Are *we* ready to order?"** or **"How are *we* doing today?"** If you mean "you," say "you," not "we." Don't talk to adults as if they're toddlers. (And—not that you asked—but it's best not to use baby talk with toddlers either.)

# READER'S CHEATSHEET FOR CHAPTER 6

To *consistently* deliver great customer service requires you to build and maintain *standards* and *systems* capable of creating repeatable results.

A *standard* can be:

- **A tactic for performing a task more easily and successfully** (at an auto repair shop operation, this might be how to put a lug nut securely back on a wheel without over-tightening).
- **A brand standard** (for the same repair shop, this could be which magazine titles to have—and avoid—in the customer lounge).

A *system* is somewhat more involved. It's *a set of actions a business executes consistently to make the experience better* for its customers. There are five categories of service systems.

- **Preparation.** Systems that help clear the way for a great service experience *prior* to its delivery.
- **Execution.** Systems that help employees *during* their customer interactions and that enable them to provide a high level of service.
- **Customer preference and experience tracking.** Systems that enhance the customer experience by making it more personally appropriate to a particular customer.
- **Recovery.** Systems for handling those times when things go wrong, for example, Micah's MAMA™ system for service recovery, detailed in this chapter (and also available via email at mama@micahsolomon.com).
- **Continuous improvement.** Systems for making future service encounters even better.

**Failures result from broken systems:** Although it's easy to blame an employee for a service failure, often problems are caused by a broken, or nonexistent, system. A rule of thumb here is that if a problem happens once, it may be a particular employee's error or simply a fluke. But if it happens more than once, the underlying system needs to be reviewed.

**Language is a system too:** It's important to systematize the language that you use with customers. Consider creating a **simple phrasebook** with preferred and discouraged terms and phrases to use face to face or on the phone with customers.

1. Every organization can benefit from setting up and maintaining service-related standards and systems. Is our organization doing this sufficiently, or is it more "catch as catch can" around here?

2. This chapter devotes some time to the importance of "language standards" for communicating with customers. Do we have language standards in place in our organization—and, if so, are they widely known and taken seriously?

3. This chapter also devotes time to the importance of tracking customer preferences and sentiment. Do we give these enough of a priority? Are our systems up to snuff in these areas?

4. This chapter stresses the importance of "service recovery," of having a plan in place/methodology for when things go wrong. Micah goes on to offer his MAMA system for service recovery. Do we have a similar approach already in place that's working for us? If not, should we adopt the MAMA system?

5. This chapter makes a point of encouraging organizations to look to *systematic* causes of customer service failure rather than jumping to blame a particular employee when things go wrong. Are we good about this? Could we be better?

Reminder: All of the reading group guides are available as a single document you can download for free at **guides.micahsolomon.com**.

**7**

# STEPFORD CUSTOMER SERVICE: AVOIDING THE DEADLY STIGMA OF INAUTHENTICITY

There aren't many people I have less in common with, lifestyle-wise, than Richard Branson, founder of the Virgin Group. He measures his dollars in billions. (I don't; I'm not that great with fractions.) He's besties with Mick and Sting and Quincy and Adele. (I'm not.) He kitesurfs with supermodels riding piggyback in a spectacular state of undress. (I don't think I *know* any models, super- or not, clothed or otherwise.) But Sir Richard and I do share a belief that customer service makes the business world go 'round. A *particular* kind of customer service: authentic service, service without the soul and personality sucked out of it.

### Informality and Authenticity

"We take an informal and antiscripting approach to customer service at all of our Virgin brands," Branson tells me, as he painstakingly prepares his British tea (anachronistically, as we're in downtown Chicago, at his new Virgin hotel). "Customers enjoy doing business with personable employees who tailor service to the customer and the customer's situation." By contrast," he says, "some Middle Eastern and Asian airlines"—here, he names names (I won't), all of them competitors to his own Virgin Atlantic international airline—"have service standards that are extremely high, but don't deliver the right *style* of service for customers today." All of those perfectly coiffed, well-scrubbed flight attendants, "who are only allowed to deliver scripted lines—employees the airlines keep around for what seems like only three years before they're replaced with another interchangeable flight attendant speaking exactly the same script—that's not what we're about and that's not the kind of service customers want today."

"'Stepford service,'" I offer.

"Exactly," he replies. "That's what I want to avoid: Stepford-type customer service."

Branson's preferences are well aligned with those of customers in today's marketplace. Consumers today are *allergic* to anything that strikes them as insincere, including a stilted, overly formal, or obviously scripted service style. They're looking for a candid, down-to-earth, even slangy style of communication from the busi-nesspeople who serve them. (I should clarify: this is what they want from *most* businesspeople who serve them. Customers still do prefer a few categories of professionals—such as oncologists, pilots, judges, and funeral directors—to retain a smidgen of formality.) No matter how caring a service provider's *actions* may be, if the service *style* comes off as artificial, it puts a ceiling on how intimate and inviting interactions can be between employees and customers.

## Eye-Level Customer Service

Take a moment to recall the stylistic service flourishes of the past, such as you'd encounter at great department stores like Marshall

Field and at grand hotels—tea at The Plaza during the *Eloise* era and so forth, with the white gloves and the faux-French (or BBC-meets-Buckingham Palace) accents, and the towel over the arm. This model of service doesn't sit well with customers today. It comes off as snooty and stifling, as too mothball-scented. It's also a bit nerve-racking for the customer, this "feeling that the guest and the employees are always expected to be on their best behavior—like when you're going out with your grandparents," as service designer Tim Miller puts it, "which is not the feeling customers are looking for in service at any price point today."

As a positive counterpoint, listen to how a young customer describes a service encounter she enjoyed in a Melbourne coffee shop, where she had what she called a "high-level, intelligent, mutually respectful conversation" with the barista. "He seemed on a par with me, and my feeling was that we enjoyed each other as a result."

I asked her what she meant by the two of them being "on a par."

"It felt like we were social equivalents, even though *he* was pouring the coffee, and *I* was paying him to pour it. It was comforting—and comfortable."

This young but well-traveled customer is helping me in making an important point: today's customers tend to be most comfortable with service staff being in a position of relative equality with customers, rather than standing below them in a subservient manner. Although employees should be courteously deferential and eager to please, many customers today are most at ease when employees project the attitude that "we're all in this together," the server and the served. Think of it as a "peer-to-peer," "eye-level," or "side-by-side" style of customer service.

Striving for a comforting, informal style of service is an approach that works today even in the most luxurious and pricey settings, including the double-Five Star, double-Five Diamond, triple-Michelin-starred Inn at Little Washington. One of the reasons that the Inn has thrived and continued to grow for more than forty years is that it strives to push back against preconceived notions of what a fine-dining restaurant should be. According to proprietor Patrick O'Connell, "We actively work against this [set of preconceptions], at least where it feels false and insincere to us." This isn't always easy, says O'Connell. Because his restaurant and inn are perceived as being "fancy," new employees tend to put on airs, starting on their first day of work. O'Connell tells me, with an amused twinkle, "Often, if waiters arrive here after having worked at another restaurant, for the first hour or so they strut around with that towel over the arm, and I want to say to them, 'Which bad old movie did you see that you're trying to copy? Was it from the fifties? You don't need to do that here. What you *do* need to do is put people at ease, take care of people, and make people comfortable in how you act and in the language that you use. The fancy airs that might have been cool at your last gig aren't cool here, because they're silly and artificial. *We don't want an imitation of a waiter. We want the genuine article.*'"

"If we go back in time," says Isadore Sharp, the founder and chairman of Four Seasons Hotels and Resorts, "the luxury market traditionally came with a sense of formality, of dress and mannerisms that were meant to represent a higher level of society. Companies [in the luxury sector] brought with them a connotation of formality, good manners, etiquette, etc. I look at service differently. I feel that you can still be a great host without all those trappings. You can still convey the same kind of hospitality, of welcoming, of making sure that guests are treated in a manner that is respectful. People who come into the hotel perfectly manicured and dressed to the nines should feel comfortable, as should the person with a baseball hat turned backward and a pair of jeans."

## Out with the Scripts, in with Your Own Words

In most settings and industries, I suggest you do away with word-for-word scripts. Replace these scripts with a simpler punch list of points that need to be covered in the course of conversations that have a particular agenda—for example, an agent booking a spa appointment may need to cover details such as what the guest should expect from the session and how the parking validation system works—but that employees are free to cover in their own words. This approach avoids running up against customers' innate dislike of being read to from a canned text.

*(Note: There are contexts in which this advice should not be applied, including life-and-death settings such as specialty pharmaceutical delivery, and interactions that have regulatory, privacy, or security implications.)*

Instead of training to a script, a better approach in many contexts is to train employees in dealing with both simple and complex situations. Provide them with insights that will help them to recognize different customer behaviors and situations and to respond appropriately and effectively. Relying on scripting doesn't afford you this type of flexibility. "Hospitality has to be a dialogue," says Danny Meyer. "It cannot be a monologue. If you say the same thing, the same way, to every single table, you're conducting a monologue. You're not appreciating that every table wants to be treated differently."

Not that this type of flexibility is easy to train for or to accomplish. "It takes an awful lot of practice to come across as completely unscripted," says Sara Kearney, an executive with the Hyatt organization. "We don't script, but we do an awful lot of role-plays and dress rehearsals to help people understand their role in bringing the brand experience to life."

## You Are(n't) What You Wear

The best sartorial approach, by and large, is to have employees dress in a manner similar to, or just a little bit better than, how your customers dress—at least than how your customers dress on their *non*-sweatpants days. This tends to put customers at ease and can have a similar effect on employees. Choice is also valuable here:

giving employees a degree of leeway in what they wear, while still providing them with appropriate boundaries, can help employees feel more comfortable in performing their work, and this kind of comfort is exactly what you want if you're aiming for authentic customer service interactions. (This doesn't mean you can't have a dress code or even a uniform. But it does mean you should keep the employees in mind as uniforms are designed and dress codes are implemented, and you should allow some flexibility and creativity in how they are ultimately worn.)

"Employees can't give great customer service without a great toolbox," says Richard Branson, "and when the elements of the toolbox are very personal, like uniforms, we're particularly careful to get feedback from the employees who'll be affected, before we proceed. When we make a change to our uniforms, we involve multiple employees and get their input in addition to mine.

"When I had the idea that everybody [working on his Virgin Atlantic airline] should wear red shoes, it was important that the red shoes—especially the red high heels—should fit. We spent a lot of time getting that right, because when you're on your feet all day, you're not going to give good service if you're miserable."

At this point, I had a cheeky follow-up question.

"What about *your* red high heels, Richard—how well did *they* fit?"

[If you don't know the story: once, because he'd lost a bet, Branson had to join the crew of a competing airline for a day as a flight attendant, in a skirt and high heels. He proceeded to gamely serve passengers on board all day long.]

Branson: "I found some high heels in my size at a shop the night before I did that stunt, and they fit me pretty well, thank you very much."

The business world's longstanding "tattoo taboo" is a similar issue. If you're in a corner of the business world that is still reluctant to employ candidates with visible tattoos, cheek piercings, hair colors not found in nature, and the like, I suggest you outgrow your reluctance (even if you need to do so through gritted teeth) for two reasons.

First, as an employer, you dream of *great* employees, the ones who can be empathetic and creative as they work with customers. Don't let superficialities distract you from your quest to find the employees most suited to providing great service. *Great customer-focused employees share key personality traits, but one of the things they don't share is a particular look.*

Second, letting employees revel in their own styles of grooming and self-decoration allows your company to project how genuine it is, both to employees and to the customers they support. Remember that today's customers project their own personal styles as well through tattoos, piercings, and interesting hairstyles; and, for the most part, they're okay with your employees doing the same. (There are some exceptions. For example, if you serve customers in Japan, where tattoos can be considered a gang signifier, you may want to disregard my advice.)

## Visual and Tactile Cues to Authenticity

Authenticity can be communicated to customers via visual and tactile cues at your place of business. The commercial designs and furnishings that customers today find most authentic and emotionally satisfying are a long way removed from the slick, ostentatious, overly polished commercial spaces that predominated just a few years ago. The preference today is for a preponderance of rough-hewn elements "where the hand of the artisan shows in the work and human imperfections are a part of the appeal," says Laura Romanoff, an expert in commercial interior finishes and design. (Even cooler: Laura's also my cousin.) Many customers today are turned off by over-the-top would-be status indicators such as gold leaf, crystal chandeliers, and incongruously located Corinthian columns. Gussy up your establishment with these trying-to-be luxurious touches, and the reaction of some customers is likely to be, "Do I belong here?"

## Terroir: Improving the Customer Experience by Creating a Sense of Place

A signifier of authenticity that many customers today look for is a sense of place; what I call *terroir* (pronounced tare-WAH, approximately). This is the French term for the convergence of factors—geography, climate, and so forth—that go into making a local wine or a particular piece of produce, but I use the term more broadly, as I find that the concept of *terroir* also works in other contexts to refer to whatever elements of place authentically and even quirkily distinguish one product, or business, or single location of a business, from others—whatever gives it a sense of the locale. Most any company can increase customer attraction and engagement by allowing its customers to revel in its sense of locale, like a restaurant, for example That's A Some Pizza, a microscopic (500-square-foot) Seattle-area pizzeria that disarms customers with delicious pies whose crust is made from sourdough starter dating back to Seattle's Alaska-bound Klondike Gold Rush, or even a car dealership, if it has the right vision . . .

## Howdy,* Audi! (Could What I'm Smelling in my Sweet New Ride be . . . Authenticity?)

It's true: a pleasing sense of *terroir* can actually be achieved by a local car retailer, such as the Audi Flatirons dealership in Broomfield,

---

* Reader's poll: Do you prefer the spelling "Howdy, Audi!" or "Haudi, Audi!"? Email me at goofyquestions@micahsolomon.com and let me know!

Colorado, which ties into the outdoorsy local community in multiple ways, such as by offering high-end mountain bikes to customers (so they can explore neighboring trails while their cars are being serviced). And now, the national Audi organization, Audi of North America, seeing the success of such local initiatives, has started encouraging all its dealerships to take comparable steps toward localization, "with the goal of achieving a 'sense of place' at as many of our North American dealerships as possible," says Joe Rood, Director, Service Operations and Training at Audi of America, "one by one by one."

# READER'S CHEATSHEET FOR CHAPTER 7

As a rule, the trend in customer expectations today is toward **informality** and **authenticity**. Most customers these days are put off by anything that strikes them as insincere, including a stilted, overly formal, or obviously scripted service style.

In many settings and most industries, consider doing away with word-for-word scripts. Replace these scripts with a simpler punch list of points that need to be covered in the course of a conversation, but let employees cover them in their own words.

**(Note: There are contexts in which scripts are absolutely essential, including life-and-death settings such as specialty pharmaceuticals delivery, and interactions that have regulatory, privacy, or security implications.)**

**You aren't what you wear:** Generally, it works well when employees dress more or less the same as, or just a little bit better than, their customers. This tends to put customers at ease and have a similar effect on employees.

**The tattoo taboo:** It's time to get over any reluctance you have to hiring employees with visible tattoos, piercings, or wild hair colors. There aren't enough great potential employees out there for you to let superficialities keep you from hiring the best of them because of such superficialities.

**Visual and tactile cues to authenticity:** The physical setting in which you serve customers can provide visual and tactile cues that demonstrate your authentic service style, such as design touches and furnishings.

**A sense of place:** Many of the cues that signal authenticity can be called "a sense of place" or be covered by the French term *terroir*. Many customers prefer that your business exudes a sense of place that is reflective of its particular location.

1. Is our organization's *style* of customer service one that customers perceive as authentic? For example: Does the language we use put customers at ease, or is it stuffy and overly scripted? What about our dress code, uniforms (if any), and restrictions (if any) on tattoos and piercings? Do our current policies in these areas support or fight against us being considered authentic by our customers?

2. According to this chapter, customers today tend to be turned off by finishes, furnishings, and other such cues that seem fake or sterile or ostentatious. Has our organization devoted sufficient attention to whether the publicly visible elements of our business are projecting authenticity?

3. A type of authenticity that's particularly important to today's customers in many industries and contexts is a sense of place, or *terroir*. Is this concept applicable to our organization and industry? If so, are we giving appropriate and sufficient clues to what makes us unusual (or at least specific) in terms of our location?

Reminder: All of the reading group guides are available as a single document you can download for free at **guides.micahsolomon.com**.

8

# IT'S A WILD, WILD TECH-DRIVEN WORLD (AND THERE'S NO TURNING BACK)

" **T**his internet thing," says my wife, a master of comedic under-statement, "seems to be really catching on."

Indeed.

Digital communication and the technologies that arrived along-side it have transformed our lives at breakneck speed. For everyone who makes a living by working with customers, it's essential to rec-ognize and adapt to how these forces have changed, in the course of a relatively few years, what customers want from us.

The communications, digitization, and miniaturization revolu-tions have brought technology so close to hand that it can seem nearly an extension of our own bodies. Plus, product and software engineers have worked ceaselessly to simplify user interfaces, with the result that customers are now able to expect spectacular ease of use in almost every form of technology they encounter.

In the face of such reliable, intuitive, and always-available technology, it's time to pose an uncomfortable question: *Where do human service providers best fit into the service equation today?* That is, *in which parts of the customer experience is human-delivered service appreciated by customers, and where does it just get in the way?*

Today's customers sometimes *do* want us humans to stay out of the way. Having grown accustomed to the way that online and self-service solutions can simplify their lives, they're in many contexts opposed to having human service providers gum up the works without adding value.

Consider how many transactions consumers *already* conduct every day without interacting with a single human being. They find their way to far-flung destinations without having to ask for directions; they make dinner reservations on OpenTable, then use Yelp to rate the meal when they're done; they sign up for classes, download coursework, review their grades online and afterward rate their professors on RateMyProfessors.com; they schedule and reschedule medical appointments; and on and on and on.

Until recently, each of these transactions would have required contact with at least one human being, but that's no longer the case. And, in the course of handling such transactions on their own, customers have discovered that technology can take care of some functions faster and more capably than even the best human employees could.

## Micah's (Unauthorized) Jetsons Test

For some time now, I've advocated a playful way to get my consulting clients thinking about which customer service functions belong on which side of the human/technology divide; that is, which parts of the customer experience should be offloaded to technology and which parts should continue to be entrusted to human employees. I call this mental model the "Jetsons Test," and base it on the enduring cartoon series created in 1962 but set 100 years in the future.

Here's how customer service is pictured in the Jetsons' view of the future:

*Much of the customer service is self-service and/or provided by machines:* ordering breakfast in bed from an automated menu, for example, or recording telephone messages on rewriteable LP records (I love the way they got this particular prediction at least 75 percent right). And, of course, housecleaning via Rosie the Robot, the animatronic housekeeper with a New Yawk accent and an attitude to match.

And in the Jetsons' world, *wherever service is provided by human beings, it adds the elements that customers tend to crave from a human interaction: warmth, texture, and, often, a little drama or intrigue.* Consider the friendly, Southern-accented receptionist at the factory where George Jetson works: She's not needed by the factory for her message-taking (which is handled by those rewriteable vinyl records), but her value comes every time she provides her warm greeting to every arriving visitor. Or consider Henry, the superintendent/handyman at the skyscraper apartment building where the Jetsons live, who does odd jobs here and there, but whose primary function is to be a buddy for the Jetsons family.

This is a pretty solid model for divvying up different elements and scenarios of your service delivery:

> *If a human can perform a function best ("best" here can mean more flexibly, accurately, creatively, warmly, or pleasantly), be sure to have a human continue to carry out that function. But if the task or touchpoint is something that can be handled best by automation, artificial intelligence (AI) and chatbots, algorithms, or self-service, be sure to offer the appropriate technological solution—at least as an option—for your customers.*

Where the Jetsons Test *can't* help you is where the situation is ambiguous: where warmth comes at the expense of efficiency, or vice versa. Then, it's a judgment call. And there will be *many* such judgment calls—if you're paying sufficient attention. To a large extent, the answer in these ambiguous situations is to provide *multiple* service channels for customers so they can choose for themselves if they value warmth over efficiency, or the opposite.

But sometimes you *will* need to make a judgment, bravely putting your foot down in favor of exclusively offering human-delivered service or in favor of 100 percent self-service. Here's a creative example of a company making this kind of judgment call and putting its corporate foot down in favor of human-delivered service. When Singapore Airlines redesigned the interiors of its business class cabins a few years ago, it did so in a way that the airline knew would result in flight attendants being required to *manually* provide bedtime turndown service: passenger by passenger, row by row, the flight attendants take the mattress and bedding personally in hand and prep it, even fluffing up the passenger's pillows just so—before each passenger turns in for the night.[1] (This is in contrast to the nighttime setup in some carriers' business class cabins, which are designed to work automatically and leave any pillow adjustment and sheet-straightening as the responsibility of the passengers themselves.) Singapore Airlines has chosen to retain turndown as a human-delivered service because the airline believes that it's fundamental to the experience they want to provide for their passengers: the feeling of being cared for in flight.

To go "full human" in a context like this, à la Singapore Airlines, isn't intrinsically right or wrong; rather, it's a choice, a strategy. But I do applaud the steadfastness on display here and how it contrasts with so many businesses that are doing everything they can to take human employees *out* of the equation, even where those employees could continue to add warmth and connection, for example, hotels that bribe their guests to do without housekeeping (in return for some rewards points) and the companies in so many industries that replace their long-tenured, personable telephone operators with an auto-attendant.

## MILLENNIAL CUSTOMERS: A POWERFUL
## AND UNIQUE GENERATION OF CONSUMERS

*Let me take the time here to introduce millennial customers, and to talk about how they are affecting the fortunes of businesses today and will continue to do so in the future. (Note: This section only covers millennials as customers. Millennials as employees are covered in chapter three.)*

Let me start with a story you probably *already* know. Millions of soldiers, sailors, and airmen return from World War II to the embrace of millions of riveting Rosies—actually, it seems those Rosies and servicemen found each other *very* riveting, as their reunions would result in a spectacular output of offspring over the course of only a few years. This created the biggest generation America had ever seen, and these children—the baby boomers—grew up to transform the social and economic landscape of a nation.

Now, here's the sequel to that story: *The baby boom has happened again, and then some.* The boomers themselves—the children of the WWII generation—have, in the fullness of time, given birth to the largest generation in history—one that's even bigger than that of the boomers themselves. This is true both in the United States, where the effect has been further boosted due to immigration, and worldwide, although the strength of the phenomenon varies widely from country to country. These are the millennials, also known as Gen Y, the generation born between 1980 and the late 1990s (or thereabouts), who are transforming society once again.

Now, the snarky headlines you've seen regarding this generation may have you thinking, "Why should I care about catering to millennial customers? Aren't they Top Ramen-eating, impecunious, and underemployed?"

Well, not exactly—and certainly not for long. With a wallet power that's growing quickly and will soon exceed that of the boomers, millennial consumers are rapidly becoming a *very* big deal for most companies. It's estimated that millennials will *directly* spend $10 trillion over their lifetimes and control the spending of trillions more via the positions they've been rapidly rising to within the companies where they work.

In business travel—which is an excellent proxy for a wide range of spending activity—the millennial generation will account for nearly 50 percent of all business flights in 2020, according to Boston Consulting Group. In contrast, boomers may end up accounting for as little as 16 percent of business flights the same year, and could dwindle even further—to as little as 11 percent by 2025.

I draw your attention to millennial customers *partly because of their direct economic importance, and partly because what a millennial expects today, older consumers will likely start expecting tomorrow*; millennial preferences and behaviors are rapidly spreading to, and being paralleled by, older consumers as well. Christopher Hunsberger, a renowned hospitality consultant, formerly of Four Seasons Hotels and Resorts and more recently working independently as a high-end hospitality consultant, makes this point as follows:

Millennials are an important group of customers in their own right. But their significance is more than that: They're a unique group in terms of their impact on the rest of our customer base. The behaviors and expectations of the millennial group of guests tend to shape the thinking of the rest of us.

In other words, the standard expectation of a twenty-five-year-old customer today will be paralleled by the expectations of their moms and dads and older brothers and sisters as well in a very short time. If you can please the first, you'll soon be pleasing the latter as well.

So, what *are* the expectations of these young consumers? Millennials have been shaped by a lifetime immersed in the fast-evolving worlds of online commerce, search engines, and on-the-go connectivity. Smartphones have been the norm for most of their lives. The internet has always been on. They've never licked a stamp or balanced a checkbook or called 411 for directory assistance. They've grown up at a time of great choice in almost every consumer arena; their entertainment choices haven't been limited to what's on the radio at the moment or what can fit on a CD or DVD;

and the shopping choices available to them have always been sufficiently diverse for it to seem realistic to align their shopping with their values—the chance to choose humane, green, fair trade, organic, employee-owned, and so forth.

Beyond that, *the expectations of millennial customers are essentially the same as those represented throughout this book, just more so.* In particular, they have a pronounced affinity for a peer-on-peer, eye-level style of service and a strong passion for authenticity and *terroir* (as was just covered in chapter 7); a desire for speedy service and for service that's delivered on the customer's own timetable (it's particularly easy to fall off the cliff of dissatisfaction with this demographic—see chapter 10); and the yearning for the customer experience to truly *be* an experience (as covered in chapter 5), with the happy corollary that they'll share word of experiences that move them, via social media, like nobody's business (see chapter 9).

## Jetsonizing Retail

Whatever industry you're in, there are likely Jetsonian decisions to be made: junctures in your operation where it may no longer make sense to use an old model to serve new customers, whether in hospitality with its tradition-bound front desk, or in B2B with its entrenched traditions of account management, or in healthcare where the patient experience has many traditions ripe for review.

And then there's retail, where the most glaring anachronism may be the way merchants treat customers at the end of the interaction, when the customer's primary desire is to pay and get out of the store. Let me state what should be obvious: *When a customer's trying to hand over their money, they shouldn't be forced to endure a line for the privilege of doing so!*

The point here is not just that a tablet can replace a traditional cash register. It's that many merchants will benefit from moving beyond the archaic concept of a separate queuing area—a place set aside specifically for the customer to wait in line before being allowed to pay and leave—that still holds back many retail operations. When customers are shopping *online*, they're not corralled into a standing formation until the website's ready to check them out, so why should merchants assume that they need to do this to customers in the physical world? (*Nobody* appreciates lines—with the possible exception, I suppose, of a kid at the zoo admiring the zebras.)

In other words, expand your thinking beyond the traditional model of a cash route, in which the customer goes to a *place* to do the transaction—and replace it with a setup that's more fluid and internet-like. This is the model with which the Apple Store burst onto the scene, providing an experience where the mechanics of the transaction—receipts, register, cash drawer—are kept out of view, allowing the focus to stay on the needs and interests of the customer.

While it may seem overly ambitious to model yourself on Apple (which was able to approach the issue with essentially limitless funding and technological know-how), there are affordable tools that make a similar approach possible for merchants of more modest size and budget. Let's look at how a revised setup has improved the customer experience at Camelion Design, a small, seasonally busy home design and accessories retailer in my home base of Seattle. For fifteen years, Camelion's customers were served, sometimes with difficulty, by a single cash register. During the holidays, this historically meant, at times, as many as ten or fifteen customers standing (and stewing) in line.

That was until a few summers ago, when, to be ready for the next holiday rush, Camelion installed a POS (point of sale) system, designed by Accumula Technologies and Lightspeed, to remedy the situation. It runs on three Apple devices, allowing any employee anywhere in the store to ring up customers on the spot. What's more, employees are never taken off the floor as they would be if they were staffing traditional registers. (Taking employees off the floor to staff a register has well-known negative consequences in retail in terms of sales, service, and loss prevention.) Now, when the holidays roll around, Camelion never has much of a line at all, and is able to do more business than ever while keeping customer engagement high and customer frustration low.

## HOW TUMI IS TRANSFORMING ITS CUSTOMER SERVICE TO BE AS BULLETPROOF AS ITS LUGGAGE

Whenever I'm at the airport or boarding a plane, I'll amuse myself by watching the antics of my fellow traveling businesspeople, in particular how they'll cast an envious eye toward anyone who is rolling or carrying the latest TUMI luggage. TUMI ownership provides instant elevation to cool-kid status within the traveling business tribe (at least in the eyes of the poor schlubs consigned to carrying AmazonBasics luggage), like a great lunchbox did at school in days of yore.

However, I don't recall actual lunchboxes being indestructible the way TUMI bags so clearly are. (Indestructibility, in fact, is my fundamental complaint with TUMI: that the stuff so rarely breaks or wears out that I have a hard time coming up with an excuse to buy the brand's latest, ever more eye-catching and feature-laden models.)

The premium workmanship and overall product standards at TUMI posed a challenge as well to Charlie Cole, who took over as chief digital officer at TUMI in 2016, as well as becoming global chief e-commerce officer at Samsonite, TUMI's corporate parent, starting that year. "Being known for our standards in manufacturing and style, when we do get a customer service issue"—and Cole says they get their share: logistics issues, a.k.a. "where's my stuff?"; customers searching for their refunds, etc.—"our response needs to be commensurate with the product quality, because that's what customers are expecting from us. Otherwise, in the glare of the contrast, it's going to be a real disappointment."

Indeed, when Cole came into the company, a glaring contrast is what he uncovered. "In the aggregate, we've long been known for some pro-customer fundamentals, in the sense of having a solid warrantee and standing behind the product with a great repair center, and never wavering on these. Yet we were fairly lackadaisical in our systems to handle such things, which made it hard for customers to get the service from us that they wanted, and that we wanted to provide. We weren't doing a good job of supporting that customer service in our call centers, whether on the phone or by email, because, frankly, we had amazing people on our payroll who were saddled, at the time, with mediocre tools."

## THE POWER OF BEING CHANNEL-AGNOSTIC

The most obvious place where the operation was falling down was in speed of response. Cole immediately asked, when he first came to TUMI, that everyone in the company cc him on every single inbound customer service request. "I did this for a while when I got here, and what I would see is us taking excessive and unpredictable lengths of time to get back to our customers. This wasn't a by-product of poor training, or lack of discipline, or anything else on that continuum. It was simply a by-product of the systems we were using."

The solution TUMI came up with is a new, integrated approach that allows TUMI to be channel-agnostic. "The way we sped up service to our customers was to give them more choice in channels. We didn't force customers to call us on the phone; we didn't force them to use email; because when customers are also able to use various real-time channels to reach us, like Facebook Messenger and WhatsApp, they're a lot happier, and they get the resolution they're looking for a lot sooner." With the new functionality, which is powered by the Gladly customer service platform, regardless of the channel on which the customer initiates the discussion, TUMI's agents will respond and continue the conversation on the same platform seamlessly, even in extreme cross-channel scenarios, such as if a customer starts out by sending an email, then follows that up immediately with a phone call, then, while on hold, decides to open up a web chat window.

## FROM NOW ON, YOU'RE A NAME, NOT AN ORDER NUMBER

Aside from speed of reply, Cole had also been frustrated by "the traditional way customer service operations are arranged by *order* [at TUMI and elsewhere]: 'Micah ordered this backpack on 12/1,' or whatever it may be. An improvement I wanted to see, and that we achieved with the new [Gladly-based] system, is to be able to pull up the entire customer history every time a customer calls in, in a single thread. This gives our customer service reps more actionable insight into what the customer has done with us in terms of purchase and repair history, how they have corresponded with us in the past, and what they may be looking for in the future."

All of this futuristic Jetsons talk makes me hungry, so let's talk about pizza. I'm also pivoting the discussion in a pizza-ly direction because of my *Solomon Anecdotal Theory*™. This posits that a reader's retention is improved when I include as many examples as possible that feature

a) pizza
b) puppies
c) precocious babies and toddlers

The Domino's Pizza Tracker is an app- and web-based widget that lets customers check on their pizza's progress at every stage, from the moment it's ordered until it shows up at the door. (The historian in me notes that the Pizza Tracker replaces Domino's original, spectacularly ill-conceived [they didn't ask me!] thirty-minute delivery guarantee, which proved to be an unholy terror to pedestrians and other drivers alike, leading Domino's to wisely, if a bit belatedly, cancel the guarantee.) The new approach to timely delivery that the Pizza Tracker represents offers real-time updates that demonstrate how a customer's order is progressing through Domino's five-step timeline:

Step 1:    Order placed
Step 2:    Prep
Step 3:    Bake
Step 4:    Quality check
*(I hear you snickering about this step, you gourmet pizza snobs, but knock it off! Snarkiness is beneath you.)*
Step 5:    Out for delivery

## Don't Force Them to Ask

All of which may seem like too much information, but there is logic behind Domino's approach here: As a customer, it's not only important to me *how long* the pizza takes—whether that's thirty minutes, or more like twenty-five or thirty-five. What's just as important—for my sake and the driver's—is that I know precisely *when* the pizza's coming, so that I have enough warning to make sure that I'm around—and clothed—rather than picking the wrong moment to be in the shower.

And what I most definitely *don't* want to be forced to do is to call Domino's on the phone to find out:

"Is my order coming?"

"*When* is it coming?"

"Oh no—I hope I remembered to order the breadsticks *without* cheese for my lactose-intolerant housemate. Did I?"

. . . and so forth.

In other words, the Domino's app is powerful because it's designed to give customers the information that they're likely to be looking for, *without requiring them to ask for it.* Making things effortless—questionless—is one of the most effective ways to improve the customer experience.

## THE POWER OF 360 IN CUSTOMER SUPPORT

When you *start out* working in customer support, you usually do it with the best of intentions. But it may not take long for those good intentions to get worn down to nothing if you're forced to work, shift after shift, with tools that simply aren't up to the task. As Tomas Gorny, the Nextiva CEO, explains, it's tough to "spend your workday using some half a dozen different platforms to communicate externally with customers and internally with your co-workers" or if you lack a "quick, frictionless way to access even the most basic information about a customer, let alone view more sophisticated information such as the predicted value of that customer," or even lack a view of what's *already* been communicated to the customer, without which you risk embarrassment and losses for your company:

> **Support Agent:** *"Great news! I'm authorized to gift you a $10 discount code."*

> **Customer:** *"Uh . . . your other rep, 'Marty,' just sent me an identical note but saying he's giving me a $15 discount. So I guess that means you're saying I can combine these two discounts? For $25 off? Sweet!"*

In response to such challenges, Gorny and company recently built a solution they call NextOS. NextOS provides a 360-degree panoramic view of each customer, including real-time sentiment monitoring of all customer interaction channels. NextOS offers multi-channel integration; this is the ability for support agents to communicate to customers on all channels on a single screen, and the ability to allow a customer to stay on the customer's desired channel rather than requiring them to switch channels for the company's convenience. Because all channels are essentially equal on NextOS, the agent has access to everything (email, chat, social, and

> voice) in the same place, alongside the historical details and frequently updated situational insights that allow the agent to avoid wasting either the customer's time or their own.

## Don't Wear Customers Down by Making Them Call for Stupid Stuff

It's bad form and bad business to wear customers and prospects down by requiring them to spend time and effort to contact your business for answers to the kind of questions I've become notorious for referring to as *Stupid Sh-t*™: questions that customers will likely have and that you should have *predicted* would come up. (When I'm on a consulting engagement for a client who's squeamish about profanity, I call this *Stupid St-ff*™, which is just about as descriptive.) Customers don't want to call your company to find out, for example, whether an order has shipped; they want to *already* know this via an immediate, automated email or text confirmation. Similarly, they'll be peeved if they get lost while trying to visit your office because they had to guess your physical, GPS-friendly, address, since only your post office box is listed on your website. (These are simple, even simplistic, examples; please be aware that the more technical your product or your service, the longer the list of questions that customers would consider "stupid" if they had to reach out to you for answers.) It's important to relentlessly hunt down such irritants and time-wasters for the sake of your customers. Strive to elevate the lowly concept of avoiding stupid sh-t to a high art in your organization.

## Using AI (Artificial Intelligence) to Eliminate Time-Wasting Inquiries

AI (artificial intelligence) can feel like a scary proposition when considered as an either/or proposition—as an oppositional force to human employees, including the human support agents we all know, manage, and love. But AI can help answer mundane inquiries and avoid wasting the time of both your customers and your customer-facing employees, as follows:

- AI can power a dynamic search bar on your site, answering a customer inquiry more completely and effectively than a static, and, most likely, rarely updated, list of FAQs ever could.
- If *that* doesn't solve the customer concern, AI can quickly deliver the factual information a customer is looking for via a chatbot served strategically to customers on the pages of your site where such concerns are likely to come up.
- AI can decipher a customer need and not only answer it, but *take the next action needed* as a result: for instance, generating a return label automatically.
- AI can even deliver "policy exceptions" that assist customers who have lightly stepped outside of stated company norms, such as being a day over the standard use period for a coupon or the return period for a product, perhaps deciding to make such exceptions based on the loyalty/VIP status of the customer.

All in all, the best way to think about AI is to consider it within a triangular model (see Figure 8.1).[2]

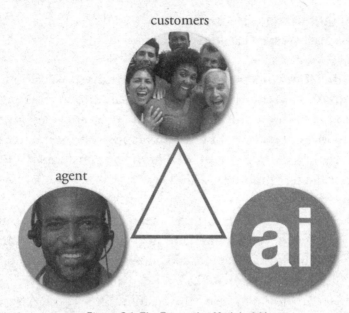

Figure 8.I. The Triangular Model of AI
Graphic © Micah Solomon, **micahsolomon.com**

At one vertex of the triangle is the customer. At the second vertex is the AI. At the third vertex is the agent. And, explains Ryan J. Lester, senior director of customer engagement technologies at LogMeIn, "truly great support comes from having, for want of a better word, a *conversation* among the three of them."

That conversation might *start* with a chatbot, or it might *start* with an AI-powered dynamic search bar. But AI can't do everything; nor will it be able to in the near future. That's where the agent comes in—not necessarily with the bot "handing it over" to the agent, but with the bot continuing to assist the agent, in one of two ways, says Lester: "The AI-powered bot can then continue to support the customer conversation, and if the customer asks a question the bot knows the answer to—the trackable status of a shipment, for example—the bot can automatically insert those tracking results into the conversation and free the agent to focus on more important things or work with more customers simultaneously. Similarly, the bot, interacting behind the scenes with the agent, can be making recommendations such as, 'Based on what the customer's talking about, I think the best approach for them is X.' Then, the agent can either insert that recommendation verbatim or reword it in a more empathic manner."

Consider this hypothetical conversation between the client of a financial institution and an AI-powered bot and a human agent:

**Customer:** "I want to roll over my IRA."

**Bot:** "I can help you with that. Here's the link where you can fill in the info for the institution and account you'd like to roll it over to."

**Customer:** "Thanks. But I see that the form you linked me to is demanding the address of the institution. But I only have their account number, not their physical address."

**Bot:** "Let me get you to an agent who can help you with this."

**Customer:** "Oy vey."

**Agent, stepping in:** "Oy vey, indeed!! Happily, I actually speak a bit of Yiddish—unlike the bot—and I can help you with this. The address is a formality but you can't leave it blank. Let's see what we have as far as addresses for your institution."

**Bot to Agent (invisible to customer):** "I find their address in Orlando at XX."

**Agent:** "We have found an address in Orlando that should work for you. We would always recommend checking with your institution, but the address we have found is an official on-record address for the external institution so it should work."

**Customer:** "I retract my 'Oy vey.' Thanks for the help!"

**Agent:** "Happy to do the heavy schlepping for you! Hope the rest of your day is wonderful."

"GET TO THE POINT, MICAH!"

# READER'S CHEATSHEET
# FOR CHAPTER 8

**The Jetsons Test:** Customers have reached a point where they some-times *do* want to handle various service transactions on their own while having human employees stay out of their way. The question, though, is *when* this is and isn't true. The Jetsons Test suggests that if a human employee can perform a function best ("best" meaning more flexibly, accurately, creatively, dramatically, or simply more pleasantly), your company should have humans continue to carry out that function. Conversely, if the task or touchpoint is something that can be handled best by technology, be sure to offer a technological solution—at least as an option—for your customers.

But there will be judgment calls with which the Jetsons Test can't help you. These are ambiguous situations: where warmth comes at the expense of efficiency, or vice versa. To a large extent, the answer in these ambiguous situations is to provide *multiple* service channels for customers so they can choose for themselves if they value warmth over efficiency, or the opposite. But sometimes you *will* want to make the judgment call yourself rather than offering both self-service and human-delivered options.

**Don't inconvenience customers by making them ask you for Stupid Stuff™: the answers to questions they should be able to find for themselves.** The technology you deploy to your customers should provide them, where practical, with the information and answers they are looking for, without them having to inconvenience themselves by asking for it. AI, to pick an important example here, can allow customers to find the answers to many mundane questions on their own and free up human agents for more interesting challenges. And there are various other solutions and approaches that can help here that are much better than an old-school, rarely updated, listed of FAQs.

**If you're a retailer, stop slowing customers down when they want to pay and leave:** It's time for brick-and-mortar merchants to stop making their customers wait in line for the privilege of handing over their money at a traditional register. There's affordable technology available that can assist nearly any size business in streamlining the customer experience during checkout to make it analogous to what customers experience online, where nobody ever has to wait in line to pay.

**The millennial generation of customers:** Millennials, born between, approximately, 1980 and the late 1990s, are the largest generation in US history and in many other parts of the world.

This generation has a wallet power that's growing quickly and will soon exceed that of the boomers.

As customers, millennials' expectations have been shaped by a lifetime immersed in the worlds of online commerce, search engines, and on-the-go connectivity. Smartphones have been the norm for most of their lives. The internet has always been available. And they've grown up at a time of great choice in almost every consumer arena.

It's important to pay attention to millennials for two reasons: First, because of their direct economic importance. Second, because their preferences and behaviors are increasingly spreading to the customer behavior of older generations. These expectations are largely the same as those represented throughout this book, just more so: In particular their passion for local authenticity (*terroir*) and their desire for an informal, eye-level style of service; their expectations for speedy service and for service on their own timetable; their passion for the customer experience to truly *be* an experience; with the happy result that they're very likely to share word of the experiences that move them.

1. According to this chapter, we've entered an era where customers have grown eager to achieve many of their goals without human intervention. Do our own customers show this growing affinity for technology-powered, nonhuman-mediated types of customer service? Or is it different in our industry from the landscape described?

2. In this chapter, Micah proposes a "Jetsons Test" to determine which functions to offer on a self-service basis and which to assign to human employees:

   *If a human can perform a function best ("best" here can mean more flexibly, accurately, creatively, warmly, or pleasantly), be sure to have a human continue to carry out that function. Otherwise, if the task or touchpoint is something that can be handled best by automation, artificial intelligence (AI) and chatbots, algorithms, or self-service, be sure to offer the appropriate technological solution, at least as an option, for your customers.*

   Has our organization been thoughtful in deciding which functions should still retain a human feel versus where our customers would prefer to serve themselves via automation and digital tools?

3. This chapter describes millennials as a uniquely large and influential generation of customers. Are millennials an important

group of customers for our organization now, or will they be soon? If so, do we have a good handle on accommodating the needs and desires of this generation?

4. This chapter portrays millennials as a bellwether generation, whose desires provide hints for what customers of all ages will be expecting in the near future, due to the infectious nature of millennial expectations, especially, but not only, in relation to technology. Have we seen this play out in our customer base—or, for that matter in our personal lives: are all of us becoming millennial-like, regardless of age?

Reminder: All of the reading group guides are available as a single document you can download for free at **guides.micahsolomon.com**.

**9**

# GOING SOCIAL:
# HOW "WORD OF THUMB"
# IS CHANGING YOUR WORLD

E very day, in almost every industry, customers are sharing in ways
that would have been unthinkable a few years ago. In retail,
customers are taking selfies in the dressing room and sharing them
with faraway friends in order to get their opinions on fit and style. In
the restaurant world, diners are sharing course-by-course photos as
their meals progress; the *New Yorker* cartoon, in which a waiter asks
a camera-wielding guest, *"May I suggest a wine and a filter setting?"*
is far from an exaggeration. Even in healthcare, tweets and status
updates from inside the ER are hardly unheard of, and getting
medical opinions via text and Twitter from far-flung friends and
family members before procedures (and sometimes in the middle
of them) has become commonplace.

Today's customers are perpetually sharing, and scouting for,
impressions of the brands and companies that interest them. They
research products and services, plan their purchases, and buy and con-
sume what catches their eye—sharing their experiences all the while.

Even if this sharing ethos is most pronounced among younger customers, it's a decidedly multigenerational phenomenon. Today's customers, of all ages, share nearly all of their consumer activities with their circle of online acquaintances as well as looking to these acquaintances for guidance on what they themselves should buy. This profoundly influences both what gets purchased and how it is then consumed or experienced.

It also means that *your customers themselves are now considered to be purchasing authorities within their social circles.* Never before have consumers enjoyed such powerful platforms to broadcast their opinions, enabling them to share their thoughts about your business both when they're prospects and again once they're actual customers.

## Help Your Customers Elevate Their Status through Social Sharing

*Why* do customers do all this sharing? A reason worth considering is that *customers share in order to elevate their status (in other words, their relative social standing).* Status these days looks different than it did in the old days of clearly gradated status increments, such as the way the car industry in Detroit would encourage customers to climb, over time, from Chevy to Cadillac to Corvette. Elevating status today isn't necessarily about spending money on something that traditionally would be considered aspirational; it can be a well-planned excursion to an isolated yurt that, for all its supposed isolation, is then shared endlessly via Instagram and Facebook. A photo to post of a superb meal at an offbeat restaurant is as much a source of pride as a physical memento (such as a souvenir menu from a white-tablecloth restaurant) would have been a few years ago.

An important way that purchases and experiences increase a customer's status in a social media context is by turning your customer into a *discoverer* in the eyes of their friends, family, and followers. As a study by the Futures Company has shown,[1] consumers are taking more and more pride in making discoveries for themselves, such as interesting products and services for sale, that result in a customer becoming recognized by their peer group for being "first." The medium of exchange, in other words, is *social currency*, which they use in building and maintaining their relationships with others. *Any effort and creativity you can invest in finding ways to help customers collect social currency will not only boost your customers' social status, it will help you build your business.*

Look at how Drybar, the blowout-bar phenomenon we met earlier, elevates the status of its customers through social media. The Drybar social media team regularly posts (with permission) before-and-after photos of their customers' blowouts on Facebook and Instagram, whereupon fans critique and comment on these transformations, in some cases selecting winners to "hang" on Drybar's wall of fame on Facebook.

The Drybar mobile app also has sharing functions built right into it. When a Drybar customer makes an appointment via the app, they're invited to share the date, time, and location with friends, who may show up as well, thus parlaying this originally solo booking into a real-life Drybar meetup. In addition, the company makes its physical spaces as shareworthy as possible, taking pains to make them photogenic for those who want to post their latest salon discovery to Instagram.

## Social Media Survival

Undeniably, this heightened sociability brings its own set of challenges and downsides. It's tricky doing business in a world where your company's every interaction with customers might be broadcast to the world. Here are five principles for social media survival that will help you serve, support, and engage with customers socially:

1. **Approach your social media response from a "customer support" point of view.**

   Customer support via social media channels is a relatively new arrival on the scene (when compared to telephone customer support, which goes back many decades, and email, which is also pretty well established), and it's often treated haphazardly in comparison. But I encourage you to put a similar level of planning and professionalism into how you approach it; you should be ready to engage and assist customers via social media as systematically and thoroughly as you do via more traditional channels.

   To get this effort off on the right foot, staff your social media team with true customer service professionals. This is better than placing employees there solely because of their affinity for technology, who may or may not have the same affinity for human-on-human interaction. Properly selected and trained customer support representatives know how to "listen" empathetically and answer in kind. This is perhaps even more important on social media than it is on the phone, due to the lack of audible cues like you'd get on the phone and the fact that your employees are leaving a written, public record with every social media response.

2. **A personal tone goes a long way.**

   The expectation on social media is that a company's representatives will use an informal, sincere, and non-corporate tone rather than standing loftily above their customers and proclaiming from on high. If your social media customer interactions sound stuffy or generic or legalistic, your customers will sniff you out immediately as a fake.

3. **Respond immediately.**

The easiest way to compound your company's social media embarrassment after a corporate misstep is to drag your feet in responding to questions and frustrations that have been posted publicly. A negative event in the online world gathers steam with such speed that the delay itself can become even more of a problem than the initial incident.

To avoid such delays, set strict company standards for how fast to respond to customers on social channels. Also, prepare for those instances where the definitive way to respond isn't immediately apparent (for example, if you need to gather more data or check with your legal department). Devise placeholder responses in advance that can, to some extent, buy you time while a more strategic response is prepared.

4. **Don't fall into a Streisand-esque social media nightmare.**

When someone uses social media to attack your business, your natural urge may be to respond in kind or even to unleash your lawyers in hopes of pressuring the attacker into removing the complaint. I beseech you to think twice before taking this route.

In the era of social media, a defensive reaction, particularly one intended to suppress a negative post, tends to bring *additional* publicity—*negative* publicity. The classic cautionary tale is that of Barbra Streisand, who once sued a photographer in the hope of getting him to remove photos of her mansion's backyard from an online databank he had compiled, a survey of erosion along the California coast. This action brought *more* publicity to the images of her backyard, rather than less. In light of the resulting interest sparked by Streisand's combativeness, a detailed photo of her backyard was reproduced on everything from T-shirts to coffee mugs—and there's now a dedicated Wikipedia page where this phenomenon has been dubbed "The Streisand Effect." Ouch.

Any social media argument with a customer represents an exponentially greater risk for your company than the old-fashioned kind of argument that happened before social media, because of the visibility and "shareability" of the medium. So, make sure that everybody who represents your company online has taken the time to learn how to breathe and to bite their tongues. And then bite them again.

5. **Take it direct.**

When you find yourself facing a negative post on a social media channel, reach out to the source directly.

How? The best approach is usually to reach out to the customer *in channel*, meaning that when a customer posts on a particular social channel, you respond on that same channel, at least initially. This can start with a simple and authentic public response (for example, a publicly visible tweet expressing your concern). But after that immediate public response, offer to take the conversation private while the two of you work toward resolution. Once you move the discussion out of a public venue and into a one-on-one setting, you can work directly with your antagonist without thousands of eyes dissecting your every move while likely failing to understand the nuances of what's going on.

Going private can be as simple as changing from public tweets to direct messaging (DM), although this can get tricky because, on Twitter, you can't DM a customer who isn't already following you. Or you can set up a special, branded private channel (there are a variety of third parties that can help a business get set up this way). The telephone is also a private, personal channel and is great for talking things through—but only if you are not seen as *pressuring* the customer to switch from a social channel to the telephone; customers today feel that brands should meet them where they already are.

## A RESOURCE FOR MY READERS

If you would like a standalone, printable copy of these five Social Media Survival principles, please let me know by email at social@micahsolomon.com.

*"GET TO THE POINT,*

*MICAH!"*

# READER'S CHEATSHEET
# FOR CHAPTER 9

Today's customers are continually sharing their impressions of the brands and companies that interest them, and of products, services, and customer experiences.

One reason that customers share impressions is to increase their own *status* in the eyes of friends, loved ones, and casual acquaintances. The medium of exchange, in other words, is *social currency*, which customers use in cementing and boosting their position in their relationships with others. If you can help your customers collect this social currency, it will boost your customers' status as well as help your business grow.

## Social Media Survival: Five Principles

1. **Approach your social media response from a customer service/customer support point of view.** It helps if you

staff your social media teams with true customer service professionals rather than with employees you've chosen solely because of their affinity for technology.

2. **Take a personable, informal tone** rather than sounding stiff and corporate when posting to social media.

3. **Respond immediately.** Time on social media moves extremely quickly, and a lag in response can exacerbate a minor incident and turn it into a fiasco.

4. **Don't bring yourself additional (negative) publicity by responding aggressively or defensively to a post that you don't like.** Specifically, you don't want to experience the "Streisand Effect" that is warned against in this chapter.

5. **Reach out to the source of negative social media posts directly,** staying in channel at first (i.e., not asking the customer to immediately switch to telephone or email). Then, after your initial, publicly visible response, offer to take the conversation private as you work with your customer toward a resolution.

1. Is our organization doing enough to make it easy for customers to engage with us and spread the word about us via social media?

2. One factor that motivates customers to share is the opportunity to *elevate their status* in the eyes of their online cohort by being seen as a "discoverer." Does our organization offer opportunities for customers to discover items/experiences ("social currency") that can help them elevate their status socially? If not, are there opportunities to do so that would make sense for us to pursue?

3. At the end of this chapter, Micah lays out a set of five pointers for what he calls "social media survival." Do these suggestions align with how we handle social media at present? If not, should we adopt these five pointers as ours?

Reminder: All of the reading group guides are available as a single document you can download for free at **guides.micahsolomon.com**.

# THE CLIFF OF DISSATISFACTION

N ext time you're feeling under the weather, you could try picking up the phone and calling Cleveland Clinic, the internationally renowned medical institution. Instead of being given the typical runaround, you'll hear the following invitation:

*"Thank you for calling Cleveland Clinic; would you like to be seen today?"*

(After 4:00 p.m., the greeting changes to the only slightly less astounding, *"Would you like to be seen tomorrow?"*)

Cleveland Clinic's move to provide same-day appointments (in place of the traditional model that required you to schedule, sometimes, weeks in advance in order to see a specialist) wasn't easy. Organizational resistance to making the change was intense, and the process and systems improvements required were daunting.

Success ultimately came through a combination of leadership resolve and clever process innovation. For an example of the latter: one of the secrets of the same-day promise is sophisticated on-the-phone triage. Let's say you call up and say, "I have a headache. I want to see a neurosurgeon." Right away, you'll be guided through a series of screening questions. Depending on how you answer them, the agent on the line who took your call will determine which kind of professional you should see and ensure that you do indeed get that same-day appointment.

However, if they determine on the phone that you have just a garden-variety headache, it's unlikely that you'll see a neuro-surgeon; more likely, you'll get face- or phone-time with a nurse who's a headache specialist. Crucially, though, if the way you describe your headache sounds more serious, you'll be hustled right in to where you need to be, says Dr. James Merlino, who headed patient experience for Cleveland Clinic when the new approach was deployed:

> If you say certain things which are warning signs– answering "yes" to, "Is this the worst headache you've ever had in your life?" is one—you will immediately be transferred to a nurse who will do more assessment and then guide you to our emergency department. Or, if you call and say, "Look, I was in my local emergency room last night with a headache; they did a CAT scan and say I have a brain tumor; I need to be seen by a neurosurgeon today," you *will* see that neurosurgeon today.

For Cleveland Clinic, the results of this initiative have been transformational. Most strikingly, many measures of patient sat-isfaction that would seem to be unrelated to speed of service have risen almost in lockstep with the deployment of the new initiative. This is not surprising. *When you succeed in serving your customers on their preferred timetable, it goes a long way toward improving their impres-sion of the customer experience overall.* So, by increasing the speed of its service, Cleveland Clinic improved patient perception of the quality of its service *overall*.

Increasing your speed of service may also help insulate your company against competitors: existing competitors as well as future upstarts. For Cleveland Clinic and other traditional healthcare institutions, this competition includes a growing threat from the walk-in urgent care clinics that will soon occupy every commercial street-corner location that isn't already inhabited by a Starbucks (or, in some locales, a marijuana dispensary). The secret of the growth of urgent care clinics isn't that they share or even *claim* to share the reputation for sophisticated medicine and wide-ranging expertise of an institution like Cleveland Clinic; it's that they offer something that traditional healthcare has long failed to provide: *service on the schedule of the patients*, service that matches the urgency of their needs and the complexities of life that represent reality for the modern, overscheduled customer.

## Beware of the Cliff of Dissatisfaction

What Cleveland Clinic was facing—and overcame—can be called "the cliff of dissatisfaction," the moment when a customer falls out of love, or at least out of patience, with a company due to slow service. The amount of time you have before a customer's relationship with your company starts teetering on the edge of this cliff varies from industry to industry, location to location, and even from morning to afternoon (for whatever reason, people are generally more impatient early in the day), but the cliff of dissatisfaction is an inherent risk in most service interactions and business relationships.

Starbucks knows how long an average customer will contentedly wait, from walking into the store until receiving a finished, customized drink. Although Starbucks dresses its stores with merchandising and interesting décor to make these minutes pass by as pleasantly as possible, the company understands that, ultimately, *too long is too long*. So, when "too long" threatens, countermeasures are taken. Baristas will venture out from behind the counter and take orders ("Can I get something started for you?") from customers who still have a long way to go to reach the counter. The company also deploys technological solutions to speed things along, including its wildly successful mobile app, which includes an option to preorder.

And ultimately, Starbucks lets the cliff of dissatisfaction guide its business expansion. As soon as the company's metrics indicate that the level of demand and the resulting wait times are threatening customer satisfaction, Starbucks opens another store down the block (or sometimes elsewhere within the very same office building—I've seen this here in Seattle!) to alleviate wait times and be sure that all customers are served in a timely fashion.

## Is Everyone in Your Industry Too Slow?

One way that a business can get lulled into a false sense of security is when the timetables of *an entire industry* lag behind the expectations of today's customers. If this is the case in your industry, it may be hard for you to recognize that you have a problem that needs to be addressed. A friend of mine tried to order furniture not long ago, only to be told that delivery would take twelve weeks. "Did you *seriously* say twelve weeks?" he replied, not snarkily—well, not *too* snarkily—but in genuine amazement, having never been quoted such a long turnaround for anything, ever. Here's the source of the disconnect: In certain industries, *twelve weeks is pretty normal*. The players in these industries haven't felt much motivation to improve—because their direct competitors are also slowpokes. I would argue that if *everyone* in your industry is too slow, it's time for *you* to be the one to revamp your field before someone—the future Uber or Amazon of your industry—does it first.

## Even When You Can't Literally Go Faster, You Can Keep Your Customers Safely Away from the Cliff of Dissatisfaction

There are, most likely, multiple steps your organization can take to improve the actual speed of your service, for example, dedicating yourselves to reducing telephone hold times, cutting down on in-person waiting, and returning emails more quickly. But even if you *can't* go any quicker, there are creative ways to align your company with the timetables of your customers. Extending your hours is an obvious one. Offering appointments, if you're currently exclusively first-come-first-serve, is another. (If you go the appointment route, try to do it in a way that requires minimal effort for the customer, such how the Apple Store lets you preschedule Genius Bar appointments via its app.) If it fits your situation, consider adding preordering options, as Starbucks does with its mobile app.

In some contexts, you should consider offering service *between times*—for a restaurant, this would mean having something available to eat for hungry customers who walk in *between* breakfast, lunch, and dinner.

In telephone support, even if you *can't* answer calls more quickly, you can still answer them on a timetable that's more convenient for the customer, by taking a page out of the playbook of thoughtful companies like Southwest Airlines that offers a callback option. This way, when a customer calling in would be faced with a long hold time, you can provide the alternative of returning the call at a time of the customer's own choosing.

Finally, in many business contexts, you can conform yourself more closely to the schedule of your customers by offering sophisticated self-service account management tools ("my account" functionality) that are available to all customers 24/7 and can provide service even after your employees go home.

## DIALING INTO YOUR CUSTOMERS' SCHEDULING DESIRES THROUGH DEEP LISTENING

In 2012, Safelite AutoGlass began an initiative to transform itself from an *operationally* focused company into a *customer-centric* one, "which we could only do by, in a sense, turning the practices that we'd previously adhered to inside-out," in other words, to look at them all over again, but this time entirely from the customer's perspective, explains President and CEO Tom Feeney. To gain this customer perspective, Safelite moved from a solely numerical vision of the customer to a textual one, to enable them to listen more thoroughly to what customers had to say. "We decided to stop worrying about the numerical Net Promoter Score (NPS) that had defined customers for us up to that point"—even though Safelite's numerical NPS was high (84) at that time and has since further risen to an eye-popping 88—"and instead pay attention to what the customer's 'verbatim' [the free-form response portion of a customer survey response] was telling us. This is a fuller, more textured way to truly be looking at our business through our customers' eyes, and a lot of what we read in these verbatims is eye-opening."

Much of what Safelite gathered from these customer comments is that it was time for the company to place a higher value on customers' time and effort, starting with their online experience. "Based on what we read in those verbatims, we became obsessive about bringing down the number of clicks required to complete the scheduling of a job with us, from forty clicks down to less than fifteen: in fifteen clicks and about three minutes, you've told us who your insurance company is, you've picked the part [windshield], you've scheduled it. And, on top of all that, we've assigned a technician to you, identified the part in our warehouse, and married the part, the technician, and your desired time and location."

Furthermore, for greater speed, ease of use and reduction of friction, Safelite made it so that an insurance company customer in need of windshield replacement never had to visit an external site to get this done, by embedding the operating engine of their own Safelite website into its insurance partners' websites. "With USAA or Progressive or Allstate, for example," says Feeney, "if you're on their website to file a claim, as soon as it becomes clear it's a glass claim, you'll be moved from the insurance company's website to the Safelite website seamlessly. It's still branded as the insurance company, but with the Safelite engine working behind the scenes to fulfill that policy holder's needs."

A third time-related digital innovation was also suggested by customer verbatim commentary. "We heard from customer after customer that 'although it's nice that you've narrowed it down to a four-hour window [from the previous eight] on the day of the appointment, what I'd *really* like to know is, thirty minutes out, the precise time you're going to be here.'"

The first stab Safelite took at addressing this was to start building what turned out to be an *excessively* automated system, based on the company's historical data for how long appointments were likely to take, married to geofencing that could determine where a technician was at any given time and the distance and traffic conditions between the appointment locations. Based on these data points, the system would send an automated notice (without any technician input regarding what was happening on the ground) to the customer predicting the technician's arrival time. However, this first stab at a solution isn't the one Safelite ultimately ended up with. "We quickly learned—and it was interesting psychologically to find this out—that technicians didn't want to be constrained by what the computer said *should* be their arrival time," says Feeney. "The technicians wanted to retain that power, that discretion. And they were more likely to abide by the commitment they themselves made to the customer than to abide by something the computer said on their behalf."

So version two—the one Safelite ultimately settled on—is *technician-driven*. An "On My Way" text message is sent by the technician telling the customer when the technician expects to be arriving and including the technician's picture and even a brief bio, to provide reassurance that the person about to show up at the customer's door is indeed a bona fide Safelite employee. Then, an Uber-like function called "Watch us on our way" becomes available to customers who want to further pin down the employee's impending arrival; this allows the customer to actually track the Safelite van traveling along the way, from the technician's prior location right up to the driveway of the customer's home or office.

## Send Your Customers a Message
## (And Let Them Send One Back)

A simple and effective way to align your customer service with the timetable of your customers is to add texting (messaging) to your mix of communication and support channels. Messaging is a form of communication that conforms itself particularly well to a customer's schedule. Plus, messaging is already wildly popular as a communication channel in your customers' *personal* lives; it's been estimated that people spend *five times* as much time messaging every day as they spend on voice calls, and this appears to be true across nearly all demographics.

Now, to be sure, text communication is lacking one attractive element of traditional telephone support. A voice telephone call includes audible cues that contact center professionals rely on to help them gauge and engage customers, and, when necessary, to defuse tense situations.

But limiting your customer communications exclusively to voice support over the telephone has downsides, and they relate to speed and time. First off, a telephone interaction often starts, inauspiciously, with the customer getting *put on hold*. Then, once the conversation actually begins, perhaps after a long and inconvenient time on hold, both customer and agent are forced to interact *right now* and only right now. In other words, once a customer has finally made it through the queue to talk to an agent and finally has that agent's undivided attention, the customer only has that attention for a single, defined stretch of time. Once the customer hangs up, they'll probably never be able to reach that particular agent again—even if there's one detail still in need of clarification that the customer forgot to bring up the first time while the clock was ticking.

The improvement that messaging offers here is a chance for the interaction to be nearly as real-time as a voice call but with more flexibility—fluidity—in how that time is allocated, thus integrating itself into a customer's life in a way that feels organic. Ryan Lester of LogMeIn, the makers of the Bold360 customer engagement suite, says he's been struck by "how enthusiastically customers have been responding to new messaging-based support options. I attribute this to the continuity of moving from the messaging they use in their personal lives to using the same to conduct business. Today's consumers are comfortable using this channel for everything from ordering a pizza to planning their next vacation. And it's only going to continue to become more mainstream."

## Auditing Your Own Business, Because You Can't Become Faster Until You Know How Slow You Really Are

To keep your relationship with customers from falling off the cliff of dissatisfaction (or to find out if it already has), you'll need to audit the current state of timeliness at your business. While this audit may eventually need to become quite involved and technical (depending on the nature of your business), you can generally start the process by conducting an *informal* audit yourself, simulating your customers' perspective in order to suss out how you're doing in relation to the dreaded cliff.

I suggest including the following five elements in your informal audit:

1. **Anyone there?** Submit an anonymous inquiry via one of your site's web forms, and try the same via mobile. How quickly does someone respond: Eighteen hours? Twenty-four hours? Never? ("Never" happens *a lot*.)

Such a lag may have been fine in the languid commercial landscape of, say, 2004, but an eighteen-hour response time feels like *years* in internet time today. *Your customer may have already moved on* before your company gets around to responding; even if they haven't, the impression that's been left is less than stellar.

2. **Check your desktop- and mobile-website user experience.** Are your "my account" self-service features as useful and intuitive as they could be? (And if you don't have "my account" functionality, you should be setting it up pronto so customers can assist themselves around the clock.) If your company offers actual commerce online, how easy and quick is it for customers to make a purchase?

3. **In person, check on whether anything is constraining speedy service.** How long are the queues to obtain service or to pay, if you still have such queues? How convenient and plentiful is parking? And so forth.

4. **Promises, promises.** Look at what happens when someone or some *thing* representing your company makes a time-based promise to a customer, whether that promise is made by a human being or by generic company messaging such as an autoresponse to a customer's web inquiry: Does your company keep that promise? If an autoresponder tells a customer that they'll hear from you "within the day," does the customer, in fact, hear from you within a day? Do your packages ship when you promised they would ship? Are the items listed as in stock actually in stock? Does your receptionist arrive in time for you to open by 9:00 a.m. as your website promises, or more like 9:07?

Furthermore, do you err on the side of the customer? For example, if your company sends out a service technician with a promise of arrival "between the hours of 1:00 and 3:00 p.m.," does the technician show up at 2:55, thus technically meeting the deadline but inconveniencing your customer for the remainder of the afternoon?

5. **If a tweet falls in the forest . . .** Also check what happens when a customer posts a question or concern on social media. You can do a preliminary test on this yourself with a trivial query like, "Am I right that only 'rich chartreuse' and not 'traditional chartreuse' is being offered as a color this spring?" In far too many cases, *nothing* happens. Or nothing will happen for much too long. This doesn't cut it with customers, particularly those who are social media-savvy, who will expect responsive and speedy interactions with the brands they patronize.

There are other touchpoints to look at as well, which can get very detailed in particular scenarios (e.g., lag times in custom manufacturing and in the building trades, insurance claims response timelines, and the like). So, eventually, you'll want to undertake a more sophisticated audit, but these five steps should get you on the right track, and they have a good likelihood of exposing some glaring issues that may be dragging you down.

"GET TO THE POINT, MICAH!"

# READER'S CHEATSHEET
# FOR CHAPTER 10

**The cliff of dissatisfaction** is the point at which a customer falls out of love, or at least out of patience, with your company due to the sluggishness of your service. The implications of this, both negative and—if you get things right—positive are broader than you'd think. *When you succeed in serving your customers on their preferred timetable, it goes a long way toward improving your customers' impression of the overall experience.*

**Even when you can't go any faster, you still can keep customers from falling off the cliff:** While the most direct way to avoid having the customer relationship fall off the cliff is to improve your actual speed of service, there are also creative ways to match the timetable of the customer even when you can't speed up your service. These include:

- Extending your hours or adjusting them to better match customers' schedules.

- Offering a callback option rather than forcing customers to languish on hold when you're busy or understaffed.
- Introducing messaging (texting) so that customers can interact with you entirely on their own schedule.
- Offering a self-service "my account" feature so customers can check on their projects and update account details even when you're closed or simply swamped.

**If your entire industry is slow:** If your *entire industry* operates on a sluggish timetable, it can lull you into thinking that your customers are fine with this status quo. This kind of thinking risks leaving you, along with your equally slow competitors, as a sitting duck when someone comes along to Uberize or Amazonize your industry.

1. The cliff of dissatisfaction is the point at which a customer loses patience with—and, quite likely, faith in—an organization because the service is too slow. Do we have sufficient ways here to monitor our speed, and how customers feel about that speed, in all portions of the customer journey? If not, should we undertake the self-audit approach offered in this chapter, beginning on page 191?

2. Is our *entire* industry too slow? An entire industry or niche can unwittingly be lulled into complacency when *everyone* in the industry is slow, leaving all players in the industry vulnerable to a potential disruptor who has a different idea of what "timeliness" means. Is this our situation? If so, should we start benchmarking our speed against speedier players *outside* of our industry?

3. Sometimes, a company *can't* go any faster but can manage to please customers by conforming to their desired timeline in other ways, for example by offering callback options when hold times would be extreme or by offering self-service account management tools ("my account" functionality) that are available to customers 24/7. Have we considered approaches such as these to better align with the timetables desired by our customers?

Reminder: All of the reading group guides are available as a single document you can download for free at **guides.micahsolomon.com**.

# DO YOU READ BOOKS BACKWARD? (IF SO, YOU'LL BE STARTING HERE.)

**D**o you always start at the *back* of a business book? If so, you're hereby busted! Though I totally understand if you do; I'm the same way. I'll often scan a business book starting from its back pages, wanting to know where the author's going to end up before I spend a couple hundred pages of my life with them. (No, I don't do the same thing with novels; I'm not a monster.)

But assuming you started my book at the beginning, and you've read it the conventional way, front to back, here's what I want to say to you upon your completion: *you're now well on your way toward achieving customer service mastery.* I feel strongly that if you read, you'll succeed: that business and personal success come to those who invest in reading, absorbing, and implementing the knowledge that's available via the written word. To that end, I've tried to do my part by infusing *Ignore Your Customers (And They'll Go Away)* with the essentials of transforming your business's relationship with its customers.

Inevitably, though, there will be an area that needs to be made more specifically applicable to your own particular industry or circumstance. If that's your situation, please don't languish in the dark. Instead, go ahead and email me directly to share some details of your business situation. This will allow me to send you a few suggestions for next steps that are specifically applicable to your own circumstances. You can use my direct email, micah@micahsolomon .com, or text/call me, if you prefer, at (484) 343-5881. There's also a live chat feature where you can reach me immediately, or within 15 minutes of "immediately," on my website, www.micahsolomon .com, that will connect you with me right away (unless I'm driving!).

Of course, I'm eager to hear from you professionally, if you think your company could benefit from my involvement as a customer service and culture consultant, customer experience designer, keynote speaker, customer service training designer and trainer, or author/influencer/content creator.* Between now and when I hear from you, I'm sending you my wishes for success in all of your customer-focused endeavors.

---

* Sorry. That list is exasperatingly long. Here's the short, digestible version: If it has to do with customer service, hospitality, customer experience, patient experience, or any other term for taking care of customers, I do it or I know someone who does.

# ACKNOWLEDGMENTS

The help that was most essential to the creation of this book came from Vandy Solomon, who both served as muse and cheerfully gave me the breathing space and support necessary to write and rewrite and re-rewrite. Many thanks as well to Yaniv Masjedi for going far, far, far beyond; Seth Godin likewise; Ari Solomon like-likewise; Lila Solomon for her work on the manuscript; Noah Solomon for inspired kibitzing; Bill Gladstone (Waterside Productions) for exceptional agenting; Tim Burgard for editing, good humor, and support; Jeff James, Amanda Bauch, Jeff Farr, and Beth Metrick for the same; Ed Miller; Bob Flanyak; Bill Quiseng; Kenichi, Kenzi, and Nancy Sugihara; Cary Wheeland; Blain Crandell, MD; Slim and Brenda Harrison; Allison Sitch; Stewart Zelman, PhD; Jack Blaine, MD; Tony Jacobellis; Scott Parr; Ryan Lester; Alison Parker; Daniel H. Pink; Portia Cooke; Herve Humler; Martha Humler; Raj Singh; Colin Taylor (he of "the eh team"); Tricia Primrose; Brenda Homick; Simon Neggers; Rose Gottwald; Tally McClain; Adam Cook; Peter Economy; Grace Sharples Cooke; Laura Romanoff; Tim Miller; Tom Feeney for the wonderful foreword; Frankie Littleford for the fabulous preface; Jason Yardley; Doug Carr; Jay Coldren for multiple contributions, including many insights and turns of phrase; the extraordinary Leonardo Inghilleri; the indispensable Jorge Krüger, Richard Isen, and Alan Dubinsky; Patrick O'Connell; James Merlino, MD; Danny Meyer; Jenny Roy; Zareen Islam; Mike Cohen; Joe Rood; Ann Alba; Barbara Cave Henricks; Nina Nocciolino; Miguel Morales; Brad Black; Raul Leal; Richard Branson; Joyce Romanoff; Greg Magnuson; Brian Badura; Irene Lui; Evan

Brubaker; Lisa Holladay; Michael Landau; Alli Webb; Hope Greig; Liam Doyle; Tim Anderson; Jeroen Quint; Daniel Hostettler; Tom Post; Loren Feldman; Tanya Klich; Melissa Mueller; Heather Paradis; Hamza; Joanna Horn; Brianne Garrett; Carlo Chavez; Ann Noder; Patrick Stoyanovich; Dan Schuman and Veer90; Paul Groomer; Scott Parr; Mike Wittenstein; Georgia Little; Ron Wingård; Lori Jo Vest; Marilyn Suttle; Roderick Wolfson; Melissa Grant; Marci Delisle; Carl Sussman; Seth Goldman; Kimberly Thompson; Panos Panay; Charlie Charlie Charlie Hunter; Bernadette Wheeler; Larry Wells; Charles Pollmar; Paul Groomer; and the companies and professionals whose examples and insights are represented in this book. In memory of Dad.

# NOTES

### Chapter 2: The Secrets of Building the World's Best Customer Service Culture—Yours

1. I first recounted this incident on p. 103 of *High-Tech, High-Touch Customer Service* (AMACOM, 2012).

### Chapter 3: Talent Management: Recruiting, Selecting, and Nurturing the Team Who Will Power Your Success

1. Susan Reilly Salgado, "8 Ways to Hire Great Employees," *Inc.* (October 15, 2014), https://www.inc.com/susan-salgado/8-ways-to-hire-for-hospitality .html.
2. Hat tip to Sting and the Police.
3. *The Deloitte Millennial Survey* (January 2014), https://www2.deloitte.com /content/dam/Deloitte/global/Documents/About-Deloitte/gx-dttl-2014 -millennial-survey-report.pdf.

### Chapter 5: The Experience Means Everything

1. I confess I lifted this quip from the brilliant John McPhee.
2. Leonard L. Berry and Kent D. Seltman, *Management Lessons from Mayo Clinic* (McGraw-Hill, 2008).

### Chapter 6: Building a Backbone to Support the Smiles

1. Adapted from *Exceptional Service, Exceptional Profit: The Secrets of Building a Five-Star Customer Service Organization*, Leonardo Inghilleri and Micah Solomon, AMACOM.

### Chapter 8: It's a Wild, Wild Tech-Driven World (And There's No Turning Back)

1. David Owen, "Game of Thrones," *The New Yorker* (April 14, 2014).
2. The triangular model was first posited by Ryan J. Lester, Senior Director of Customer Engagement Technologies at LogMeIn.

## Chapter 9: Going Social: How "Word of Thumb" Is Changing Your World

1. "The New Kinship Economy: From Travel Experiences to Travel Relationships," The Futures Company, as commissioned by Intercontinental Hotel Group, 2013 (Whitepaper).

# INDEX

# ABOUT THE AUTHOR

Photo by Danielle Barnum

Micah Solomon, President and CEO of Four Aces, Inc., is a leading authority, consultant, author, speaker, trainer, and content creator on customer service, the customer experience, hospitality, the patient experience, company culture, and culture change. His bestselling books have been translated into more than a half-dozen languages and are the recipients of multiple awards. He is a Senior Contributor to Forbes.com, and his expertise has been featured in the *New York Times*, *Harvard Business Review*, *Washington Post*, *Inc.* magazine, *Bloomberg Businessweek*, and many television networks and affiliates. A business leader and entrepreneur himself, Micah built his own company into a market leader and was an early investor in the technology behind Apple's Siri. His broad expertise touches on technology, the hospitality industry, manufacturing, the automotive industry, banking, financial services, HNWIs (high net worth individuals), retail, the patient experience in healthcare, and the nonprofit and governmental sectors.

Through his consulting firm, Four Aces, Inc., Micah Solomon and his team are available to readers of this book in the following areas of professional practice:

Keynote speaking
Consulting, including companywide customer service, customer
experience, patient experience, and company culture initiatives
Training, workshops, and training design
Book authorship/co-authorship/ghostwriting
Content creation
Expert-witness work (practice limited to customer service and the
customer experience)
C-suite level mystery shopping

You can reach Micah and the Four Aces, Inc. team directly as follows, in real-time
or near-real-time:

chat.micahsolomon.com — live chat
contact@micahsolomon.com — email
micahsolomon.com — website
484-343-5881 — text or voice